DOSAN'S WAY TO LEADERSHIP:
Love Yourself, Love Others

DOSAN'S WAY TO LEADERSHIP:
Love Yourself, Love Others

First Published 13 May 2011

Author: Suh Sang-mok, Ahn Moon-hye
Translator: John Cha
Publisher: Lee Chan-kyu
Published by: Bookorea Publishing Co.
Registered: 1 February 1998 No.105-90-11628
Address: A-1007, Woolimlions Balley, 146-8 Sangdaewon-dong, Jungwon-gu,
          Seongnam-si, Gyeonggi-do, 462-807, Korea
Tel: +82.2.704.7840
Fax: +82.2.704.7848
Website: www.sunhaksa.com
E-mail: sunhaksa@korea.com

© Suh Sang-mok, Ahn Moon-hye, 2011

ISBN 978-89-6324-113-5 03320

DOSAN'S WAY TO LEADERSHIP:
Love Yourself, Love Others

Written by: **Suh Sang-mok, Ahn Moon-hye**
Translated by: **John Cha**

Introducing Dosan's Leadership to the World

Dosan was the bright light of hope that Koreans needed and craved at a time when their lives were mired in despair under Imperial Japan during the first half of the twentieth century. With his vision and leadership, Dosan guided the Korean people through the independence movement. Korea finally regained its independence in 1945, but unfortunately, Dosan had passed away before witnessing it.

However, Dosan Ahn Chang-ho left behind an enduring legacy for his fellow countrymen, and his teachings then and now have guided Koreans improve the quality of their lives. This amazing feat was possible then because Dosan's philosophy empowered Korean people to carry out an impossible task. This book, *Dosan's Way to Leadership: Love Yourself, Love Others,* explains his leadership.

Many institutions around the world are studying Korea and its progress in the fields of economics, education, and democracy. This book will help them understand how Dosan's leadership played a key role in bringing Korea to the position of leadership in the world stage and how it can play a role today.

I wish my best for Dr. Suh Sang-mok and his comrades in their endeavor to develop the concept of Dosan's Ae Ki Ae Ta Leadership and write this important book. It will benefit the future generations in Korea and as well as around the world.

Paik Nak-hwan
Chairman of the Board
Dosan Memorial Foundation

Letter by Susan Ahn Cuddy, Dosan Ahn Chang Ho's daughter For Ae ki Ae Ta

I am delighted, and appreciative, to read this wonderful book about my father Dosan Ahn Chang Ho and his model of leadership. Dr. Suh Sang-mok found the answer to questions about leadership sitting in front of him. Ae ki Ae Ta… We grew up with this philosophy. The calligraphy hangs in my house for all who come here to see.

Dr. Suh brings keen attention to Dosan's visions allowing people to see how far ahead of the times my father's thoughts were. He presents a clear look at facets of Dosan's life many people are not aware of. I am happy it is in English so people outside of Korea have an opportunity to grasp the value of my father's legacy.

When I saw the first draft I called Dr. Suh on the phone and told him how excited I was to see his work. I'm grateful at 96 years of age I had the opportunity to read such a well-defined description of my father's thoughts. I am also grateful to know that his story has been told with a modern sense so a new younger generation has this chance to experience Dosan. As I near the end of my journey it is uplifting to know this book will kindle my father's spirit once again.

Leadership, or should I say good leadership, was something Korea needed desperately during my father's time. Before and after the Japanese took control of Korea, Koreans had no concept of civic responsibility and no real sense of democracy. Dosan was the person who came along at that point in history and understood why Korea lost the ownership of the country. He clearly identified the lack of leadership and the lack of qualified people to be leaders as Korea's biggest obstacle to being recognized as an independent nation. He dedicated himself to learn how to become a good leader and to teach other people how to become good leaders. He did so by example with honesty and integrity. And he did it with love. He loved Korea. He loved people.

He loved life. It is a shame his life was cut short.

All of the Ahn children were born here. My family grew up in America as immigrants with Korean heritage who had no country to go back to. My father was gone most of the time. People told us "He is not just your father, he is the father of Korea." As we grew up we realized this was true. We knew he was a man who many people sought out. But, we did not know how important he was until later on. He was always the man speaking the strongest and everyone faithfully listened to him. We could see he was a leader. He took on that responsibility wholeheartedly.

I think by Dosan's example we learned how to be leaders. We all did things in the community and had meaningful careers. We were always doing things for Korea and for Koreans. We worked in America for the independence movement and were active in its activities. And, we all served as American citizens in the armed services or working for the good of the country. My oldest brother Philip was in the US Army and became a famous movie actor in Hollywood and was involved in American and Korean politics. My next brother Philson was part of the Tiger Brigade and became a successful engineer managing a department of Hughes Aircraft. I joined the US Navy and became the first Asian woman in the Navy, the first female gunnery officer, the first Asian in Naval Intelligence and on to head the Russian Department at the National Security Agency. My sister studied chemistry and became a successful businesswoman in Los Angeles. My youngest brother Ralph joined the US Navy. He was a great athlete. He became a teacher, a coach and the Athletic Director of a high school in Los Angeles. He still works as an actor. I think Dosan would have been proud of all of us. Whatever my father taught us in the short time he was with us he taught us to do the right thing and to do our part.

Another person who taught us a lot about leadership was my mother. She was one of the first Korean women to come to America. There were no other Korean women here to teach her how to live. She went to work cooking and cleaning. She worked in a hospital. She worked as a farm laborer. And, when Dosan was home she supported him completely. And, she raised five kids by herself. As the community grew she was the woman the others came to for advice on how to live in the Korean community and with the outside community. She became the president of a patriotic woman's group. Her vigor to survive taught us how to be strong and deal with life as it came our way. She was so sturdy. Without her Dosan could not be the leader he needed to be.

As I said I am grateful there is a new spark in Dosan's legacy. Look around today. Good leadership is needed greatly. I hope people learn some insight into good leadership from my father's concepts. Ae ki Ae Ta is an idea we can all grasp. Although Dosan's commitment to Korea took him away, I treasure the short time we had together. Throughout my life I have learned from him. And, I am still learning, thanks to the efforts of Dr. Suh Sang-mok.

Susan Ahn Cuddy
Lieutenant, U.S. Navy(Retired)

Table of Contents

. . . .

Preface

In the city of Riverside, California, about forty miles east of Los Angeles, three statues stand in the heart of downtown. These statues portray Mahatma Gandhi, Dr. Martin Luther King, Jr. and Dosan Ahn Chang Ho, three men who dedicated themselves to helping people.

One might ask why are they there; what do these men have in common? It is simple. They sacrificed themselves for ideals larger than themselves. Most of all, these three historical figures sought freedom for their people who suffered injustice under the harshest of circumstances. The people of Riverside were wise to honor these three men with statues, adopting them as their own for all ages.

Gandhi and Dr. King are well known worldwide for their leadership in the struggle for freedom and human rights. Lesser known, but no less significant, is

Dosan Ahn Chang Ho.

Dosan was a resident of Riverside during the early 1900s when Riverside was the center of California's booming citrus industry. He was a humble laborer from Korea, picking oranges on citrus ranches in the area. He provided leadership for his fellow workers as their labor negotiator and community organizer. Dosan taught his fellow workers "Pick each and every orange as carefully as if your country's independence depended on it." By referring to orange-picking as a patriotic act, he added spiritual value to what otherwise would have been mere backbreaking work in the blistering heat of Southern California. The laborers felt they weren't just picking oranges; they were helping their homeland recover its sovereignty. They believed in Dosan's theory that, by showing Americans how industrious and efficient Koreans were, they could win the respect of Americans, thereby enlisting their help to gain freedom from Japan. As a result, Korean laborers turned in the best citrus crops among all the labor groups. Again, Dosan showed them how by doing it himself. In short, he "walked the walk" and harvested the best and the most oranges at the citrus ranch.

Besides being a citrus laborer, Dosan was also a

freedom fighter for Korean people whose homeland had been overtaken by Japan in 1905 and colonized by Japan in 1910. From Riverside, he went on to Shanghai and became the acting Prime Minister and Minister of the Interior of the Provisional Government of Korea in 1919. He provided much needed leadership for Koreans during their long, arduous fight for independence from decades of Japan's oppression, torture, murder, plundering and cultural cleansing until 1945, when WWII ended with Japan surrendering.

Because of his powerful oratory skills, it was natural for Dosan to gravitate toward politics. However, he was capable of much more. We learn from his leadership that individuals make the difference, and he spent a great deal of time and effort developing personal improvement for Koreans. He built schools, formed groups for the purpose of cultivating character and organized communities.

Dosan was a remarkable leader. He called for individual cultivation of character and practiced what he taught, actively training himself in character building. In Riverside, what convinced his fellow laborers to do their best in picking oranges was his leadership by example.

He also wrote the words to the Korean national anthem in order to foster patriotism; taught it to his students and followers; and sang the song himself — even while under arrest in Japanese prisons.

This book is about leadership training, Dosan's way. I am not proposing that we sing the national anthem in prisons. I am recommending that we learn from his message of love, love for his countrymen and his country. His patriotism was based on a concept of genuine love, the same kind of love one feels for his or her mother. While he was in prison, he wrote a calligraphy containing four characters, Ae Ki Ae Ta, and sent it to his family in Los Angeles. His message to his family was "Love others as you [would] love yourself" and this message is the foundation for his leadership philosophy.

I have been involved with the Dosan Memorial Foundation since the 1990s. I feel very fortunate to have had the opportunity to learn about Dosan's leadership. Such leadership's true value lies in the fact that his vision and thoughts are still germane today, seventy-two years after his death.

Normally, we think of Dosan as a great patriot and nationalist, but I believe there is more to him than just that. We should look beyond his iconic stature and study and learn from the details of his leadership. Then we can apply this knowledge for the purpose of educating and improving ourselves and others.

Leadership studies began around the mid-1930s when Napoleon Hill and Dale Carnegie published their bestsellers, *The Magic Ladder to Success and How to Win Friends and Influence People,* respectively, which focused on personal success in pursuit of happiness and (mainly) wealth and fame.

Scholars in the field of management and administration followed, formalizing the study with the scientific approach. They generated analysis after analysis in the name of efficient management for public and private entities. Leaders utilized this data to operate their organizations. Performance of individual members was measured according to their productivity and efficiency. Financial reward and recognition were the prime motivational factors for the members to be more productive and more efficient.

In recent years, more people are motivated by personal happiness. They want to feel that they are leading a meaningful life, offering their time, effort, and money to good causes such as education, the environment, and helping the sick and poor. Success in life is no longer measured by wealth and fame alone. Many consider that feeling of accomplishment, hope for mankind, and love are more important than wealth and fame. Realizing this change in attitude, leadership studies have turned attention to the emotional component of the success equation, especially in the service sector of society. The concept of "service leadership" or "servant leadership" was developed based on the philosophy that assisting the members of the organization to do their work is more effective than issuing orders from the top down, as in the "power leadership" concept.

From the service leadership point of view, I think Dr. King, Gandhi, and Dosan represent the best of the Twentieth Century leaders. They all had huge impacts on leadership by serving their people. They even sacrificed their lives for their people — leaving an everlasting impact.

As I said earlier, the world is more familiar with the accomplishments of Gandhi and Dr. King, while Dosan's accomplishments are relatively unknown. Therefore, the focus of this book will be on Dosan's life and teachings to explore and learn his concepts of service leadership, especially his Ae Ki Ae Ta concept, and how to apply them toward the good of humanity.

I would like to thank Governor Kim Mun-su of Gyeonggi Province for lending his support to this project — the development of Dosan's leadership philosophy and principles for the purpose of educating the youth of the world as well as the general public.

I would like to thank Dr. Paik Nak-hwan, chairman of the Dosan Memorial Foundation, for his interest in the study of Dosan's leadership, and for his encouragement to undertake this project.

I would like to thank prominent Dosan scholar Dr. Lee Myung-hwa for her advice and assistance. Also, I would like to thank President Lee Chan-Kyu of Bookorea Publishing for accepting this project, and Huh Jeong-hoe for his help in editing the Korean text.

I am very grateful to John Cha for translating the Korean text into English. I would like to thank Dosan's grandchildren, Christine and Philip Cuddy for their help with editing the English text.

Suh Sang-mok

Dosan Ahn Chang Ho statue, The City Plaza, Riverside, California

Mahatma Gandhi statue, The City Plaza, Riverside, California

Dr. Martin Luther King, Jr statue, The City Plaza, Riverside, California

Why Should We Care about Dosan Leadership Today?

Peter Drucker (1909–2005), prominent management expert and consultant, predicted that the 21st century would be a century of management, and that leadership would be at the heart of management. I agree with him wholeheartedly. Throughout my career as a public servant, manager, and politician, I saw time and time again that management execution was the key to the success or failure of a project. Interest in leadership grows more as time goes by, and leadership education has become a prerequisite for CEO's and managers, and for young people dreaming of becoming leaders.

There are thousands of theories and books on the subject of leadership. It takes a lot of effort to wade through them. I was not sure what was worthwhile to read or study. I was in such a quandary as I researched the countless materials produced over the years. One day I realized that the answer was right in front of me all along. The answer was Dosan and his teachings about leadership and character.

Why Dosan?

First of all, I learned that Dosan's view of leadership was based on his philosophy regarding the sense of ownership and love — the same elements that everyone in the leadership field is talking about now. Dosan's leadership concept was founded on both Eastern and Western philosophy. His concept reflects the sound character that Dosan had built throughout his life by acting on his principles. His leadership principles are deeper and richer than mere theories or empty words because they are intertwined with the actual events of his life.

Like anywhere else in the world, many say that the biggest problem Korea is facing is leadership, or lack thereof. According to a recent poll in *Mae Il Kyung Je (Economy Daily) Newspaper,* 90% of the writers and journalists who are influential in forming public opinion responded that there was a leadership problem in general in Korea; and 88% of them said that political reform was necessary in order to solve this problem.

It seems that this same condition had existed during Dosan's time, the early 20th century. We can see that he had a very rational view of the leadership crisis at that time. When people said: "There are no leaders in Korea," Dosan replied: "I ask those who bemoan how we lack leaders — why don't they study and seek training to become leaders themselves?" He further pointed out that a leader was nothing special — just someone who is a little more advanced than everyone else in the group. He lamented: "The reason we cannot produce leaders is because our jealousy precludes us from the thought of growing leaders, not because we lack qualified people."

I had a chance to visit Beijing and Shanghai around 1988 when China was in the full swing of pursuing an open market policy, vis-à-vis the planned socialist economy it had been employing for decades. I was surprised to see that the Chinese leaders were very interested in economic development in Korea, and that books on President Park Chung-hee (1917–1979) were on their must-read list.

However, President Park was not very popular in Korea due to the negative view that he had been a barrier against the overall democratic progress in Korea. On the other hand, the Chinese were praising Park as the main force in providing the "Miracle of the Han River" and studied his leadership style.

I, also, had an opportunity to attend a symposium held in Taiwan in 1985 on the subject of "Comparison Analysis of Industrial Policies between Korea and Taiwan." Korean participants expressed their envy over Taiwan's market-driven policies that were unencumbered by extensive government interference. On the other hand, pre-eminent Taiwanese economist T.C. Tseng expressed his envy over Korean policies that backed Lee Byung-chul, founder of Samsung, to make a bold investment in the chip manufacturing business. He lamented, "There's nobody like him in Taiwan." In Korea at that time, everyone criticized Lee for jumping into this risky business. Even the World Bank and other financial experts around the world warned that the move was risky and suicidal.

As it turned out, Lee was right about chip manufacturing and other investment opportunities in the electronics field. Today, Samsung has surpassed Sony and become the top producer of electronic goods; and President Park Chung Hee's export policies provided the stepping stone for Samsung and other Korean companies to grow and prosper. It is now obvious that both Lee and Park made a huge contribution toward the economic growth of Korea, yet at the time when they were proposing these ideas, negative criticisms far outweighed any positive support. In this regard, Dosan was correct in his view that we like tearing down leaders instead of recognizing them as leaders.

Democratization has changed the way we conduct ourselves in the fields of politics, business, and even family affairs. Traditional "power" leadership is no longer useful. Instead, leaders must persuade and inspire the members of their community or organization. The Age of Information is upon us. Due to democratization of information, the concept of leadership is rapidly changing. Traditionally, a leader was considered to be a person with superior qualities, someone to whom we looked up to as a hero. Today, leadership studies show that anyone can become a leader, just as Dosan said about one hundred years ago, that we should not bemoan that there was no leader, but endeavor to become one.

Also, heroic deeds or ability is not the requirement for today's leader. Rather, an ideal leader is considered to be a genuine person, someone who leads by setting examples, and someone who can work together with others. In other words, the latest leadership education emphasizes the importance of fundamental human qualities; again, Dosan talked about these same qualities a century ago.

The words "servant leadership" and "service leadership" first made their appearance in the 1970s, signaling the shifting paradigm in leadership concept. I must point out once more what Dosan had said long before the 1970s — "I am here to serve you." He advanced the idea of Ae Ki Ae Ta (love others as you love yourself) as the fundamental principle for producing genuine service type leaders.

Dosan's main theme for Ae Ki Ae Ta is the sense of ownership and love of an organization or country. An owner takes the responsibility for his organization or country the same way he would for his home or family. Love is the foundation for all human relations. Without love it is difficult to serve others in the organization or country.

It is clear that today's leadership experts are talking about the same servant spirit that Dosan showed. It behooves us to study Dosan's spirit not only for the benefit of Koreans but for all people around the world. I believe that we have a budding leadership model in Ae Ki Ae Ta.

Before we get into the details of Ae Ki Ae Ta, we should become familiar with Dosan's background. Born in 1878, Dosan Ahn Chang-Ho devoted his life to Korea's independence movement until the day he died in 1938.

In 1896, Dosan graduated from the Miller Academy, a school run by Christian missionaries in Seoul, where he began his work as a community activist. He made his first public speech in 1898 at age twenty and went on to become one of the most impressive orators of the time. He founded the first school in his hometown when he was twenty-one (1899), and at age twenty-four (1902) he went to America to study the Western educational system. He continued his community activist work in San Francisco, where he formed the first Korean organization in America, the Korean Friendship Society, in 1903, which later in 1905 grew into the Kong Nip Hyophoe (Mutual Independence Association) and published *Kong Nip Shinbo*, the first Korean newspaper in America. He improved the quality of life for the Korean community in America by teaching them to clean their homes and plant flower gardens around their homes.

He returned to Korea in 1907 for what was supposed to be a brief visit. There, he organized the Shinminhoe (New People's Association), a secret society designed to be a resistance movement against Imperial Japan. He also organized the Young Student Association, forerunner to the Hungsadan (Young Korean Academy). The darkest period in Korean history began with the advent of the Japanese annexation of Korea in 1910. Dosan fled to China, where he and his colleagues planned for an independence movement. He travelled through Siberia, Europe and England, and then crossed the Atlantic to New York and on to San Francisco. He met with patriotic groups of Koreans along the way and organized their independence activities. In 1912, he became the president of the

Central Congress of the Korean National Association (KNA), an organization that would serve as the quasi-government for all Koreans outside of Korea. In 1913, Dosan launched a mission to grow leaders for Korea's independence movement and founded the Hungsadan in San Francisco. The Hungsadan (Young Korean Academy) still exists today.

On March 1, 1919, Koreans initiated a two-month long non-violent patriotic uprising across the Korean peninsula rejecting Japan's occupation of their country. Japanese soldiers put down the uprising by cruel and violent means, leaving about 7,500 dead, about 16,000 wounded, and about 52,700 incarcerated.

Dosan left his family behind in America and went to Shanghai in April 1919 in order to help organize the Korean Provisional Government. He served in two positions, one as the Minister of the Interior and the other acting as its Prime Minister. He resigned his posts in 1921 and focused on building the Assembly of Representatives and the Great Independence Party in order to consolidate all efforts related to the Korean independence movement.

He was arrested in Shanghai in 1932 on suspicion

of conspiracy in the Hongkew Park bombing incident that killed a Japanese general and injured many other Japanese officials. He was transferred to Korea as a criminal and sentenced to a five-year prison term, found guilty of violating the Peace Preservation Law imposed on Koreans by Japan. He was released from Taejon Prison after two-and-a-half years in 1935.

In 1937, Japanese police again arrested him, along with over one hundred of his colleagues, again for violating the Peace Preservation Law. He was incarcerated in Seo Dae Mun Prison. On March 10, 1938, he passed away in Seoul. The endless years of hardship and torture had taken their toll.

Considerable research has been done about Dosan and his legacy as an educator, philosopher, and independence movement activist. However, very little research has been done in terms of his leadership. The only study on record is a seminar held in 2004 under the title of "Dosan Ahn Chang-Ho's Leadership." This is unfortunate because when we scan the leadership arena, a leader of Dosan's caliber is very rare to find. Dosan's determination to develop leaders and teach them by example is unusual. It is surprising that his theories on leadership are more advanced than much of what is being taught today.

In Section One, we will survey Dosan's philosophy from the point of view of modern leadership theories; we will examine his educational methods and results, and then analyze his own actions that reflect his leadership philosophy.

In Section Two, we will look at Dosan's leadership from the perspective of personal development, relationships with others, and organization management.

In Section Three, we will go into the details of Ae Ki Ae Ta and its main theme, love. We will look into the reason why leaders are paying attention to the subject of love. We will examine how we can advance the concept of Ae Ki Ae Ta into the modern world; examine positive results that Ae Ki Ae Ta produces; and summarize a list of tasks for Ae Ki Ae Ta leaders.

Finally, the Appendix section contains a chronology of Dosan's leadership activities and some of his writings related to leadership.

Dosan and His Leadership

Dosan, citrus ranch in Riverside, circa 1912

1
Evolving Concept of Leadership

Leadership has been a subject of great interest since the beginning of time. Many scholars have researched and written numerous books on this subject. Thousands of research papers have been produced since the 1930s. Amazon.com's title listing shows more than 370,000 books under the word leadership. What is important, however, is the fact that the concept of leadership has changed according to the times and the existing conditions that changed over the years.

The Greek philosopher Aristotle argued that people could be grouped into "leaders and followers" from the time of birth, which led to Plato's theory of "governing by the wisdom of philosophers." Similarly, Chinese philosophers Confucius and Lao Tzu favored governance by holy men. This concept lasted until the mid-twentieth century, when scholars began to challenge the "leaders-are-born-not-made" theory, the Trait Theory, because common traits among the world's leaders were difficult to identify and formulate into a theory. Scholars argued that leaders could be developed through training.

Thus the Trait Theory gave way to a "behavioral approach," which defines the leader as "someone who chooses to take appropriate actions as required by prevailing situations, thereby demonstrating his or her leadership quality."

The "behavioral approach" developed further into the "situational method" during the 1960s. This new concept stated that ideal leadership could be applied in various forms depending on the situation. For example, neither the charismatic leadership of the early twentieth century, nor the participatory leadership that was popular during the 60s and 70s can prove their effectiveness in all situations. Rather, effective leadership shows up in various forms depending on the needs of the situation. In order to understand the ideal leadership form that falls within the guidelines of the "situational method," we need to consider the changing environment of the 21st Century. The 21st Century is marked by its blazing speed of change. Successful organizations are noted for their ability to effectively react to the fast changing environment in technology and competition. Given this situation, a good leader should promptly recognize the changing trends and initiate appropriate changes for his organization and its members. This approach is called "transformational leadership,"[1] It is also called "creative leadership" because changes require creative thinking.[2]

The present era is often referred to as an intuitive era. Today, IT technology facilitates instant communication and quicker decision making. Decision makers let the computer deal with analysis of information and then choose what "feels" right to them. Intuitive sense becomes very important in decision

---

1) Burns, James MacGregor, *Transforming Leadership*, New York: Grove/ Atlantic, 2003.
2) Kim Kwang-woong, *Future Leaders: Creative Leadership*, Thinking Tree (Saeng Gak ui Namu), 2009.

making, perhaps more so than logic at times.

Thus, leaders are required to possess a healthy Emotional Quotient (EQ) in addition to a healthy Intelligence Quotient (IQ). According to psychologist Daniel Goldman[3] and his study of top managers of major corporations, leaders share a common trait. He reported that 85% of them recorded that EQ was more important than IQ in their leadership qualities, and, thus, he advanced a new theory, "Primal Leadership."

Leadership training first began as an educational tool for acquiring necessary skills to succeed in business and other disciplines. Napoleon Hill and Dale Carnegie represent this school of leadership. Hill, a former reporter who also was an advisor to President Franklin Roosevelt, interviewed steel giant Andrew Carnegie (1835–1919) and other successful industrialists and wrote a book about personal success and how to attain it.[4] Dale Carnegie (1888–1955) developed his theories based on his study of a variety of people like teachers, salesmen, and others who left a mark of their own on

---

3) Goldman, Daniel, *The Primal Leadership*, New York: Brockman, 2002.

4) Hill, Napoleon, *The Magic Ladder to Success* (1930), *Think and Grow Rich* (1937).

society.[5]

Then, an explosion of MBA schools among American universities focusing on effective organizational management happened. This discipline in management became significant in leadership education. Main players in leadership education like Warren Bennis, Stephen Covey, Kouzes & Posner, and Tom Peters view leadership studies with scientific objectivity. Their purpose is to apply the measurable results of their studies for improving the effectiveness of management.

Kouzes and Posner[6] conducted a 20-year study to develop new practical approaches to management. Setting credibility as the essential ingredient of leadership, they came up with five practices of what they call "exemplary leadership." They are: Model the Way, Inspire a Shared Vision, Challenge the Process, Enable Others to Act, and Encourage the Heart.

Warren Bennis[7], a long-time business consultant

---

5) Carnegie, Dale, *How to Win Friends and Influence People*, Simon Schuster, 1936.

6) Kouzes & Posner, *Leadership Challenge*, John Wiley & Sons, 2002.

7) Bennis, Warren & Burt Nanus, *Leaders*, Goldenowl Publishing Co., 1985.

to governments and industries, emphasizes the importance of transformational leadership. He is noted for his quotes — "Becoming a leader is synonymous with becoming yourself." "Excellence is a better teacher than mediocrity." "Trust is the lubrication that makes it possible for organizations to work."

Stephen Covey[8] wrote his well-known book, *The Seven Habits of Effective People*. He is a proponent of "leadership by principles." His fundamental principles are trustworthiness of an individual and trust among people.

There are a host of other experts on the topic of leadership. As sensibility and spiritualism are emphasized in leadership qualities, pastors and popular writers have become bestsellers of leadership books, For example Joel Osteen[9] is a paster and Rhonda Byrne[10] is a TV producer. What is interesting is that their treatises on leadership are founded on values like love, trust, honesty, integrity — the exact elements that

---

8) Covey, Stephen, *The Seven Habits of Effective People*, Grimm Young Co., 1994.

9) Osteen, Joel, Your Best Life Now, Warner Faith, 2004.

10) Byrne, Rhonda, The Secret, Afris Books, 2006.

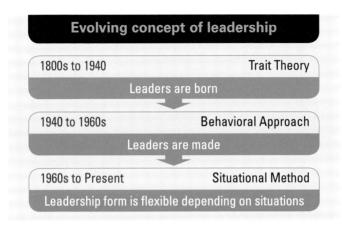

Evolving concept of leadership

1800s to 1940	Trait Theory
Leaders are born	

1940 to 1960s	Behavioral Approach
Leaders are made	

1960s to Present	Situational Method
Leadership form is flexible depending on situations	

Dosan Ahn Chang Ho advocated to his countrymen one hundred years ago. His "Ae Ki Ae Ta" teachings, literally translated, "love yourself, love others," continue to resonate today and should become a major force in training future leaders.

2

Dosan, Pioneer in Leadership

Dosan Ahn Chang Ho was a rare individual who was very keen on leadership at a time when its concept was barely established. He wrote an article called "Prerequisite for Forming Unity: Leadership" for *Dong Gwang magazine* in 1926. An orchestra must have a conductor, he states, a tour group follows a guide, and governments must have responsible managers. For any group or organization to work properly, leadership is crucial.

> "A leader is an absolute necessity if we are going to function as a harmonious group who trust each other in pursuit of common interests. An individual who

acts on behalf of his own interest may not require a leader per se. But a group or an organization, big or small, must have a leader in order to achieve its mission."

Dosan's article on "Leadership", August 1926

Next, Dosan explains who should be the leader. A leader does not have to possess a perfect set of qualifications. He just needs to be better informed in relation to the members of his group. Accordingly, if the group is composed of low caliber people, its leader may be a low caliber person with a little more knowledge than the rest of the group. Likewise, if the group is made up of high caliber people, its leader needs to be just a little more knowledgeable than the rest.

> "If we say that no leader possesses the qualifications to be a leader today, then there will not be any qualified leaders one hundred, one thousand years from now. On the other hand, if we can see that there would be qualified leaders in the future, that means there are qualified leaders today. Those who say that there is no leader today probably do not understand what a leader is."

Thirdly, Dosan emphasizes the fact that the idea of leadership should not conflict with the concept of equality. He asserts that a leadership position is not rooted in authoritarianism. A leader sacrifices himself for the good of the group and upholds democratic principles.

> "A hero is nothing special. Anyone who works with an attitude of a hero can be called a hero. There are people who do their heroic deeds whether they get credit for them or not. We have these heroes among us. They quietly do their work for our countrymen,

devoting their money, knowledge, time, and passion despite all the interferences they face. They are our heroes, our leaders. They are around us. I see people like this. You must see them, too."

Fourth, Dosan argues that there are leaders among us, but jealousy and envy prevent us from recognizing them as true leaders. He says, "That is one of our shortcomings. We tend to bring down and criticize our heroes," citing the cases of 16th century naval hero Admiral Yi Soon-shin and 19th century social reformist Yoo Gil-joon as examples.

"We seem to try to topple anyone who is capable of leading us because we are afraid to put him in the leadership position. The case of Admiral Yi Soon-shin is a prime case. He was one who should have been supported and followed, but our predecessors, out of their jealousy, conspired to make him fall. In modern times, Yoo Gil-joon was suited to become our leader, but our predecessors ignored him."

Fifth, Dosan testifies that true leaders devote all of their wealth, knowledge, and passion on behalf of their fellow countrymen and he emphasizes that such persons exist.

"I am not sure how many, but there are honest people. They are genuinely motivated to work for their fellow countrymen without committing any fraud. Also, there are those who appear to be so-called troublemakers but they carry on with their work with fairness and harmony for the good of the society, despite the constant criticism and plots against them."

Sixth, he presses the point that in order to recognize a leader and install him in the leadership position, the members of the society must get rid of their individual jealousy and take on the responsibility as an objective owner of the society.

"In order to become the person who observes the society with cool objectivity in search of its leader, one must shed all his useless vanity and take on the responsibility as an owner of the society who thinks and behaves for the good of the society. Any head of a household would be happy to see a member of his family become an outstanding person of significance. He would not be jealous."

Seventh, Dosan advises us to analyze a potential leader, his thoughts and actions, with more objectivity than we would use for an average person. He cautions us about making rash judgments based on false information or hearsay.

"Do not use vanity as a basis for accepting a person as a leader. Rather, research his principles, his character, his views, and capabilities, and determine whether you agree with them. If you consider his attributes are more superior to yours and others, then you can recognize him as a leader. Do not rely on hearsay or rumors that go around. Study carefully the record of his actions."

Finally, Dosan urges that once we select a leader, we should support him so that he can perform the job he was asked to do, and, that we should forgive his small mistakes.

"Once we recognize his talents and install him as our leader, we should not reject him in the event that he makes minor mistakes in his speeches or his actions. It is more important to try to correct his mistakes and let him do his job."

Dosan is considered a pioneer in advancing the idea that "leaders can be made through training" during the early 1900s, while the Trait Theory in leadership studies persisted until 1940s. Dosan said in a Hungsadan speech, "The reason we do not have leaders among us is because we do not train to be leaders. There are people who lament that we have no leaders. Why don't they train to be leaders themselves?"

Further, Dosan shows us how to train to be a leader. He begins by asking us to build our character, as well as improving our physical strength. First, establish the foundation of "wholesome character and healthy body," then acquire the knowledge necessary for leadership, mainly his educational principle of "deok (德, cultivation of virtues), che (體, physical training), ji (知, knowledge acquisition)."

> "There's only one way to develop many leaders in our country. Everyone must make up his mind to be a leader and study to become one. That means everyone is going to build his character to become a good person. At the minimum, everyone must cultivate deok-che-ji in order to attain qualifications to become a member of a nation."

Conditions for True Leadership

① A leader is an absolute necessity for achieving cooperation.
② The leader of a group is someone who is better informed than the rest of the group.
③ The idea of leadership does not conflict with the concept of equality.
④ Jealousy and envy prevent members from recognizing true leaders.
⑤ True leaders devote themselves in earnest.
⑥ Consider yourself as the owner of the organization when you select your leader.
⑦ Analyze the leader's thoughts and actions with objectivity.
⑧ Once the group selects a leader, they should support him or her. Forgive small mistakes.

He said this in a speech to the Hungsadan (aka Young Korean Academy), an organization he founded in order to develop leaders. He founded the educational entity in San Francisco in May, 1913, long before leadership studies came into being. This is another reason that he is considered the pioneer in leadership studies. He instituted "mu shil" (pursue the truth) and "yeok hang" (rigorously act on it) as the basic principle for the organization.

Well-known experts in leadership studies today espouse similar philosophies. Kouzes and Posner name "honesty" as the foremost quality in leadership because honesty and credibility go hand in hand.

In an article, entitled "Deceit and Honesty," in *Dong Gwang magazine* in 1926, Dosan wrote "Deceit is the root of defeat, and honesty is the foundation for success." He told his students at Dae Sung School:

> "Lies! Lies are the enemy that killed my country. I'll never tell lies again to my dying days; I'll never uphold the enemy of my Lord and father."

Further, he wrote that "being honest means assessing all matters based on their cause-and-effect, followed by meticulous planning and organizing events toward achieving specific goals; and giving it an honest

Dosan's article on "Honesty", September 1926

effort without veering from the said objectives."

He tells us recognizing the truth is not enough. Acting on the truth is just as important, no matter how insignificant it may seem. "Small truths add up to big truths. And do it today, not tomorrow." In a speech to the Hungsadan, he said, "You act on it, I act on it, we all act on it," as he made reference to the importance of acting on independence movement work.

Further, he urges us to do our best, never haphazardly. He told his helpers building his house in SongTae, "Haphazardness destroyed our nation. Even if we do our best, it may not be enough to achieve our goal. How could a haphazard effort accomplish what

Dosan's article on "Ownership", June 1926

takes a thousand years to accomplish?"

Taking responsibility for one's actions is another important aspect of Dosan's leadership. He explains his concept of "taking ownership" in an article entitled, "Are You an Owner?" The true concept of ownership means that one serves by steadily carrying out his work with a sense of responsibility for the group, not out of self-aggrandizement.

"The young, the old, the juniors, and the seniors … everyone blames his predecessors for the ills of the country. And why is that? Why don't you bemoan your own inability to bring independence to your country? Why do you blame everyone else, and not

Dosan's article on "Cooperation", May 1926

yourselves?"

Next, Dosan always emphasized the importance of a united front and cooperation. He pointed out that the greatest weakness for a nation of people was its inability to unite, saying, "United we live, divided we die." He meant for his people to unite in order to achieve certain goals together in real terms, not settle for mere emotional convention.

Specifically, this means that each person comes up with his plan of action and presents it to the group, which then goes through the process of natural selection by way of the survival-of-the-fittest principle.

Dosan's article on "Love", June 1926

Thus, the group eventually adopts the best plan. This process exemplifies Dosan's way of building democratic coalitions.

Finally, Dosan's leadership principles are based on love and affection. He proposes the idea of fellowship as an ingredient to meld members of an organization together. He defines fellowship as a mother's love for her child and her sympathetic heart for sharing her child's pains and pleasures. He urges us to practice fellowship and has specific suggestions for us — do not interfere in other people's matters, respect others' individuality, do not invade other's freedom, keep the trust, respect manners. He says, "Fellowship is paramount in generating harmony, harmony causes interest/fun, and that leads us to success."

Dosan's Principles for Fellowship

① Do not interfere in other people's matters.
② Respect others' individuality.
③ Do not invade others' freedom.
④ Do not put one's trust in materialism.
⑤ Application of fellowship varies according to the nature of relationship, i.e., between parents and children, husband and wife, and the relationship one has with friends and colleagues.
⑥ Keep promises made to each other in order to maintain fellowship.

"We as a nation of people need to interject more love into our lives. Love between parents and children, love between husband and wife, love between colleagues, love for our work, love for our organization, love for all humanity.... Lack of love is another reason why we have such a difficult time uniting together.... So let's study how to love.... Let's love fellow Koreans. Let's forgive our faults; let's praise each other for the good we do."

3

Dosan, Teacher of Leadership

Dosan devoted his life to developing leaders through his philosophy and belief. He personally established three schools during his lifetime. He built

Teachers and students at Jeom Jin School

the first school, Jeom Jin School in 1899, when he was twenty-one. It was an elementary school, the first private co-educational school in Korea. Jeom Jin means "advancing steady and deliberate" and also implies continuous preparation for the independence of Korea.

Dosan founded his second school, Dae Sung School, in 1908 when he was thirty years old. Located in Pyongyang, Dae Sung School was considered the best middle school in Korea with the best facilities and faculty, attracting high-caliber students from all over the country. Korea was not divided into North and South then. In addition to the Pyongyang campus, Dosan originally planned to open schools similar to Dae Sung throughout Korea, but this plan was cut

Dae Sung School insignia

Dosan's name card from Dae Sung School

Teachers and students at Dong Myung Academy. Dosan is seated 9th from right.

short because he had to escape from the Japanese police who were trying to stop his nation building projects. Dae Sung School and Osan School (built by Yi Seunghoon) were known as the major training grounds for developing young patriotic nationalists. The Japanese police shut down Dae Sung School in 1912 because of its pro-Korean activities such as the students' refusal to honor the Japanese flag.

Dosan's third school was Dong Myung Academy in Nanjing, China. Founded in 1924, the school prepared Korean students who were on their way to study in the United States. Many Hungsadan members at Dong Myung studied the English language and Korean history. Dosan chose Nanjing for the school because it was part of his plan to build an "Ideal Village" in this area that would be used as a model for community development in Korea after independence from Japan was achieved.

Young Students Association newspaper *"So Nyun"*

Besides the schools in Korea and China, Dosan founded a number of organizations in America which were devoted to the development of capable leaders. In 1903 he formed the "Korean Friendship Society" in San Francisco, California to help assimilate and improve the community of Koreans living there, and to organize their ginseng business. He established the "Kong Nip Hyup Hoe" in 1905. Dosan organized this first politically active group of Korean immigrants in order to bring together the different Korean communities in California and Hawaii for the purpose of supporting the independence movement. This group published and printed the first Korean newspaper in America, the *Kong Nip Sinbo* (The Independence Newspaper).

When Dosan travelled back to Korea in 1907,

he organized the Shinminhoe, an underground organization established to resist the Japanese takeover of the Korean peninsula. This organization was influenced by the developmental strategies of the Freemasons. As part of the Shin Min Hoe youth movement, Dosan formed the Cheong Nyun Hak Woo Hoe (Young Korean Association), the first Korean youth organization and forerunner to the Hungsadan (Young Korean Academy).

When he returned to America in 1911 after escaping from the Japanese police in Korea, Dosan continued to develop organizations and leadership training programs. In 1912 he organized Dae Han In Kuk Min Hoe (The Central Congress of the Korean National Association) which represented all Koreans living outside of Korea. He founded the Hungsadan in San Francisco in 1913, which continues to function

Hungsadan flag and meaning of its colors
Yellow: Mu Shil (pursuit of truth)
Red: Yeok Hang (act on it vigorously)
White: Choong Ui (loyalty)
Blue: Yong Gahm (bravery)

today as a character and leadership development institution. He outlined the purpose of the Hungsadan as follows:

> "The purpose of this organization is to foster fellowship by uniting loyal men and women who pledge Mu Shil Yeok Hang (pursuing the truth; acting on it vigorously); to train ourselves according to the three educational principles, namely *deok-che-ji* (cultivation of virtues, physical training, knowledge acquisition); to formulate wholesome character and build a sacred unity; and to prepare young Koreans as the foundation for leading our nation to achieve greatness."

Dosan sought to train and develop leaders for modernizing and reforming Korea by founding the Hungsadan (Young Korean Academy). Its charter directly reflects his educational philosophy. Yi Kwang-su, who wrote one of Dosan's biographies, conveys Dosan's thoughts on education — "Knowledge without virtue energizes evil; knowledge without physical health breeds malcontents." Yi adds further, "The Hungsadan is Dosan's lifetime work and it upholds his founding principles for his independence work, as well as putting his principles into practice." This organization's standards were high. The Hungsadan had very strict rules and requirements for membership.

Dosan himself designed the Hungsadan flag's goose image to represent unity and fellowship as well as the symbol of leadership. Geese fly together in a group heading in the same direction. When the leader gets tired another takes its place at the head of the flock continuing to lead in the same direction. The leader also makes it easier for the followers to fly as its wings' movements create more lift for the rest of the flock to

Dosan, the Teacher of Leadership

Establishing Schools
- Jom Jin School: 1899
- Dae Sung School: 1908
- Dong Myung Academy: 1924

Organizing Leadership Training
- Youth Scholars Society: 1909
- Hungsadan (Young Korean Academy): 1913
- Ideal Village Concept: 1923 and on.

Forming Leadership Organizations
- Korean Kong Lip Association (Mutual Independence): 1905
- Shinminhoe (New Korea Association): 1907
- Korean National Association: 1912

fly easier. Dosan had a keen sense about showing people what he thought.

4

Dosan, the Practitioner of Leadership

Other than Jesus, Buddha, or Confucius, it is rare to see a prominent leader actually practice Dosan's principles of Mu Shil Yeok Hang and his concepts of ownership, cooperation, and love. However, Dosan was a rare statesman who actually carried out his own philosophy.

His Mu Shil spirit is exemplary of his legacy. An exceptional orator, he poured his energy into raising funds for the independence movement. He was responsible for managing the large fund of hard earned patriotic donations; and, Dosan maintained the trust of the people he was serving through his meticulous accounting of all the contributions he raised to support the independence movement.

In his work, Dosan spent much time traveling and being away from his home and wife, but he always remained a faithful husband, never once accused of philandering. There is a famous story about a woman admirer who snuck into his room late one night in Shanghai. Dosan knew about her amorous intentions, but he did not respond to her advances. He asked her, "Did you lose something? There is a match and candle on the table. You should use them to find what you lost." Embarrassed, the woman fled, and later confessed what happened. According to Yi Kwang-su, she promised Dosan, "From now on I will serve my nation as my lover and husband," and she left Shanghai for Europe to study.

At Dae Sung School, Dosan emphasized integrity among his students and he set a strict standard of behavior. One day a student altered the roll call sheet to falsify his record of attendance. Dosan discovered the dishonest act and expelled him despite objections from the entire faculty. He insisted, "We cannot tolerate any cheaters at Dae Sung School. I want our country free of cheaters someday." He constantly reminded his students, "Never tell a lie, even in death"; "Do not lie, even as a joke"; "Repent, even if you dreamt that you compromised your integrity". He taught his students the merits of Mu Shil in specific terms — "keep your promise" and "be on time."

Sometimes, Dosan's strict adherence to his own ideals caused serious trouble for him. He had promised Lee Man-young, leader of the Boys Club, two *wons* for a club function. Two *wons* were about two dollars in 1932. It so happened that Dosan went to the French Quarter of Shanghai to see this boy on the day Korean Patriot Yoon Bong-gil bombed a Japanese military celebration in Hongkew Park in Shanghai, killing a Japanese general and wounding many other officials. The entire city was in an uproar as the Japanese police hunted down Korean leaders. Dosan should have stayed off the streets, as he was warned. Despite this tense situation, Dosan insisted on seeing the young boy because of the promise he had made to visit him. He was arrested by the French police at the boy's home. The French police then turned Dosan over to the Japanese police and he was arrested. Dosan paid a heavy price for keeping his promise to the boy, but the incident shows us how important integrity and loyalty were to Dosan.

The idea of ownership (or proprietorship) is an important element in Dosan's leadership ideology. Under this concept, an individual regards himself or herself an owner of the organization or the group to which he belongs. As an owner of the organization, he or she willingly participates and sacrifices himself or herself for the benefit of the organization, thereby becoming a leader by serving the organization. He often spoke of serving the people. "I'm not here to be your head. I came here to serve you."

Lee Yoo-pil's house in Shanghai,
French quarter where Dosan was arrested by French police, 1932

He demonstrated his idea of service to others in San Francisco, in 1903, when he gave up his own education in order to help the struggling Korean community there. He was alarmed by the unruly, shabby lives his fellow Koreans were leading at the time. Therefore, he decided to help the others instead of pursuing his studies. First he cleaned their homes and planted flowers around their yards. Soon they began cleaning their homes themselves and thanked young Dosan for showing them how. He proved to them that the simple act of cleaning positively influenced their outlook on life. Earlier, we talked about his leadership in Riverside, where he taught his

'Ideal Village' site in Philippines

fellow laborers, "Pick every orange as if your country's independence depended on it," and showed them how to do it. Through Dosan's leadership, Korean laborers consistently produced the best crop of oranges and became favorites of the American ranchers in the area.

During the formation of the Provisional Government of Korea in Shanghai in 1919, Dosan did the most work but yielded the top leadership positions to Syngman Rhee and Yi Dong-hwi. He preferred to take a back seat and serve the organization as the Minister of Labor; even though he established the Provisional Government with the money he raised in America and

Dosan arranged welcoming ceremony for Syngman Rhee in Shanghai, 1920

developed the political structure of the organization.

Dosan's "leadership by serving" is also demonstrated in his relationship with Syngman Rhee. Dosan pointed to Rhee's *yangban* (noble class) family background and his academic achievement (Ph.D. from Princeton University), and supported him as the top leader for the independence movement. Dosan installed Rhee as the head of the Provisional Government and worked hard to calm down his young colleagues who strongly opposed Rhee. On the other hand, Rhee had always been jealous of Dosan and his Korean National Association (KNA) organization, and manipulated its Hawaiian branch to secede from the KNA national umbrella, instigating division among its members. Further, Rhee regarded Dosan as his political foe and falsely accused him of being a Bolshevik, which in turn prompted the US government to consider Dosan a communist. The US investigators tracked him down in Chicago in 1925 and interrogated him. The investigators found Rhee's accusation to be false. In these incidences, one can see the difference between these two men — Dosan tried to do what he thought was best for the independence movement. He sought to serve the Korean cause, while Rhee sought to serve himself and garner personal power, true to Rhee's lifelong concept of power leadership.

Leadership expert Kent Keith classifies leadership into two types. One is the "service model" out of respect for the members of the organization, and the other is the "power model" by which the leader rules the members by authority. Machiavelli's autocratic methodology is an example of the "power" leadership model, which he devised in order to survive the combative political climate in fifteenth century Europe. He writes in his book *The Prince*, "It is better to be feared than loved" as a leader. Similarly, *Han Bi Ja* (written around 200 B.C.), considered the Asian equivalent of Machiavelli's *The Prince* in terms of its contents, suggests that "Intelligence and wisdom may not be sufficient to conquer a commoner, but power and authority conquer intelligent people."

Kent Keith points out some problems associated with the "power model", i.e., obsession with acquiring power and securing it rather than striving to use the power for the good of the whole organization. The problem is further exacerbated by the ensuing struggle

Comparison between power leadership and service leadership	
Power Leadership	Service Leadership
Control members with power	Serve the members of the organization
Emphasize seizing power (Principle of using power)	Emphasize utilizing power (Principle of using love)
Priority for ruling class	Priority for overall organization
Conflict between ruling parties	Cooperation between ruling parties
Distrust toward ruling class	Trust toward ruling class

for power among its seekers.

On the other hand, the "servant model" is based on moral foundation, and the corresponding power structure is but a tool with which to pursue the good of the whole. In this model, the power is a "gift" rather than the final objective. Accordingly, people naturally favor the servant model, and Robert Greenleaf, originator of the servant leadership model, suggests that in order for the servant model to succeed, there must be "love" among the parties engaged in formulating such an organization. In effect, Greenleaf reached the

Interior of Song Tae residence, Dosan's bedroom, 1935

same conclusion that Dosan had reached seven decades earlier.

In terms of the Korean political landscape during the days of the independence movement, we have two differing leadership styles, servant leadership represented by Dosan, and Syngman Rhee's power leadership. In the case of Syngman Rhee and his followers, they succeeded in rising to positions of power, but Korean people in general rarely respected or loved them. Conversely, Dosan and the servant leaders had difficulty in attaining power, but they commanded the respect and love of the people and continue to do so even today.

We cannot talk about Dosan's leadership without talking about "love." What impressed him in his travels throughout the West was the smiling face of the Westerners. He loved the word "smile," according to Yi Kwang-su, and he intended to post a sign "Bing Gu Ray" (the Korean word for "smile"), on a post at the entrance to his Song Tae Sahn Jahng (Mountain Villa) residence. In his famous "Words for My Comrades," he writes, "Why is our society so cold? I don't feel any warm energy. We must build a society which smiles with sincerity."

Dosan's tombstone, words by
Yi Kwang-su, 1938

Yi Kwang-su wrote on Dosan's tombstone, "He always treated people with love." His love for his comrades is exemplary. When his colleague Yi Gap was laid up with a serious illness in Siberia, he borrowed three hundred dollars from his wife, all of her savings from her housecleaning and sewing jobs. Dosan sent the money to Yi Gap in Siberia. He always looked after his colleagues, such as Lee Dong-nyung, Lee Shi-young, Pi Cheon-deuk, and Yoo Hyun-jin when they fell ill. Choi Hee-song, Dosan's colleague from Shanghai, recollected, "Dosan was diligent in paying visits to his friends' homes. He enjoyed friendly discussions with his comrades. Sometimes he liked playing the Korean chess game. Everyone who came in contact with him felt warmth emanating from him."

Yi Kwang-su commemorated Dosan on his grave stone in Mangwoori :

"He loved learning and
Accumulated wisdom
All for recovering our nation.
He loved teaching
Virtue and words
All for serving the people.
Honest, genuine,
He treated people with love
Like a warm spring breeze.
He devoted himself to his work
For the good of the public, not the individual.
He depicts the dignity of the autumn frost.

Philip Jaison (Suh Jae-pil) wrote a column in *The New Korea (Shin Han Min Bo)* memorializing Dosan:

"Dosan Ahn Chang-Ho was a man of high morals and very talented in organizing. An idealist in his thoughts and actions, yet he did not overlook the realities of daily living. He always was very devoted to his friends, but he did not tolerate those who defied principles that he regarded as sacred. He was kind hearted, but he did not compromise his principles. Dosan Ahn Chang-Ho did not go to college, but he

Dosan (right) and Suh Jae-pil, 1925

Dosan, the Practitioner of Leadership

Mu Shil Yeok Hang
- He dedicated his life to high moral values.
- He had no tolerance for deceit.
- He always backed his words with his actions.

Sense of Ownership and Unity
- He demonstrated his willingness to tackle difficult jobs, from cleaning bathrooms to picking oranges.
- He yielded high positions to others and assigned difficult jobs to himself.
- He endeavored to bring harmony between the left and the right and pursued unity.

Fellowship and Affection
- He favored words like "smile" and "bing gu ray."
- He was a good listener and a considerate person.
- He helped his colleague Yi Gap when he fell ill. He treated people with love.

learned a great deal through his school experience. His wisdom, bravery, and self-discipline surpass those of anyone with a college diploma. His heart was filled with lofty altruism, the best of his character. He learned patience in his struggles, and he believed in God's final judgment."

Ten Elements of Ae Ki Ae Ta Leadership

愛己
愛他

島山

Dosan's calligraphy Ae Ki Ae Ta, date unknown

In the previous section we learned that Dosan'
s concept of leadership consisted of the same elements
that are addressed in the modern leadership literature.
In this chapter, we will break down Dosan's elements of
leadership into ten categories and analyze each item in
detail. They are:

1. Self-examination and discovery
2. Dreams and setting goals
3. Pursuing truths
4. Developing good habits
5. Leadership by selfing examples
6. Sense of owership
7. Love and Fellowship
8. Leading the reform
9. Sharing together
10. Uniting goals

Items 1 through 4 deal with the elements
concerning "love of self" (Ae Ki); items 5 through 7
relate to "love of others" (Ae Ta); and items 8 through
10, "love of nation(or organization)."

Ten Elements of Ae Ki Ae Ta Leadership

1
Who am I: Self-examination and discovery

↓

2 **Set goals** Determine own path	—	3 **Pursue truths** Leadership of truth	—	4 **Develop good habits** Leadership by cultivation and training	**Love** of **Self**

↓

7 **Treat others with Love** Leadership of love & share	—	6 **Serve with sense of ownership** Leadership by ownership	—	5 **Set examples** Leadership by action	**Love** of **Others**

↓

8 **Lead reformation** Transformation leadership	—	9 **Share with others** Democratic leadership	—	10 **Build consensus** Cooperative leadership	**Love** of **Organization**

1
Love of Self (Ae Ki)

Dosan Ahn Chang-Ho put great emphasis on a simple truth — all things begin with self. He had three dreams. They were: gaining independence from Imperial Japan; establishing economic prosperity for Koreans; and building a nation respected by the people of all nations. To attain these goals, he strongly believed that each individual had to strive to reform himself.

"If we are to reform our nation, we must reform every one of us and each one of us must engage in self-reform. Nobody else can do it for us."

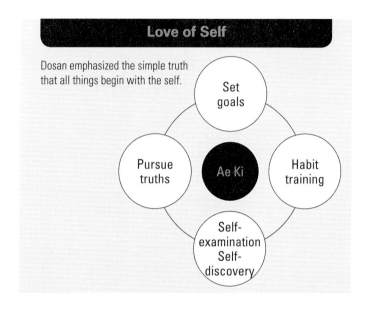

Love of Self

Dosan emphasized the simple truth that all things begin with the self.

Set goals

Habit training

Ae Ki

Self-examination Self-discovery

Pursue truths

1.1 Who Am I? Self-Examination and Discovery

I am the master of my life, nobody else. If I don't understand myself, I can't understand other people. I can't love others if I don't love myself. Thus leadership development must start with the discovery of self.

Who am I? What are my strong points? What are

my weak points? What's important to me? What do I want to be? These are some of the basic questions one must be able to answer. A lot of people think that they know themselves, but often that is not the case.

In order to know myself, I have to examine myself thoroughly. It is also important to know how others see me and how I influence them. I must have complete understanding of myself before I can begin my training process to improve my strengths and to correct my weaknesses.

Self-examination is the way to find our value system. Once we find our value system, we can set our goals. Our value system guides us in determining what is right for us and what is not. Also, a well-defined value system is a good tool to find commonalities with others and garner support from them. So finding what's important for us and establishing an appropriate value system make up the foundation for our leadership. Dosan thought that self-examination was the key for Koreans to understand who they were; what their value system was; why they fell under the Japanese rule; and how they could recover their nation. His own self-examination led him to conclude that Korea's plight

Who Am I, Examination of Self and Development

- Leadership begins by discovering one's strong points and defining one's value system.

- Dosan's pursuit of reform and new value system:
  ① From deceit to truth
  ② From artificiality to conscientiousness
  ③ From empty words to action
  ④ From coldness to warmth
  ⑤ From division to unity

was caused by "lack of collective strength and power." Wherever he went, he exhorted his constituents, "we must build our strength." He believed that national strength could be built by developing young leaders and devoted his life toward achieving that goal.

Also, Dosan discovered flaws in the Korean character through extensive self-examination. He found sophistry took precedence over simple truths, perhaps due to several hundred years of Confucian influence over people's behavior. He looked deep into the Korean psyche and determined that truth and honesty were the values that the country needed the most, and, that he could use these values to bring people together. He had realized his goal now and initiated a movement to reform the nation of people. He believed that individual reform led to national reform and began a personal campaign with the message of truth and honesty across all the segments of the society.

1.2 Attaching Meaning to Life: Dreams and Setting Goals

German writer Goethe once said about dreams, "Whatever you do or dream you can, begin it. Boldness has genius and power and magic in it," suggesting that we can set our own dreams as big as we want. This means that people with big dreams achieve big things, and vice versa. In 1953, Yale University conducted a poll for its students recording their goals in life. These results were sealed in a time capsule to be opened thirty years later. They opened the capsule to find that those students who had set goals for themselves were leading their lives among the top 5% of the population. About 80% of those who had not set goals were muddling along as an average person despite their prestigious

The Reverend Dr. Martin Luther King, Jr. A man who dared to dream.

degrees from Yale. We learn from this example that setting goals and following through with these goals make the difference in determining success and failure.

Dr. Martin Luther King, Jr. dreamed that someday he would live in a nation that would judge his four children on the merits of their character, not the color of their skin. He died before seeing his dream come true. His dream came true forty years later in 2008 when Barack Obama was elected President of the United States of America. At Grant Park in Chicago on the night of his election Obama said, "If there is anyone out there who still doubts that America is a place where all things are possible, who still wonders if the dream of our founders is alive in our time, who still questions the power of our democracy, tonight is your answer."

Dosan also had a big dream — the independence

of Korea. He told a Japanese prison guard, "All of the Korean people believe that they will achieve independence, and so they shall. World opinion says that Korea will gain its independence, and so it shall." He died without seeing his dream come true,

Barack Obama fulfilling his dream

but Korea gained its independence seven years after his death.

He had other dreams for Korea. He said in a speech to a group of young people:

"There will be the time when our Tae Geuk (Korean) flag will wave in cities across the globe. Our flag will represent absolute trust and superb quality. I must say we Koreans are in a shameful situation right now, but some day the word "Korean" will be synonymous with virtue, wisdom, and honor. It will be entirely up to our own efforts to achieve this great honor."

At the time when Dosan spoke of this particular

dream, everyone probably thought that he was out of his mind, since the possibility of realizing such a goal seemed so remote. However, as it turned out, his vision was not that far off. What he saw eighty years ago has become reality. Korea now commands serious respect around the globe as a member of the Organization for Co-operation and Economic Development (OECD) and G20, as one of the major economic powers of the world.

For Dr. Martin Luther King, Jr. and Dosan Ahn Chang-Ho, their dreams came true long after they passed away. Their dreams were not based on short term personal gain, but on a long term vision for the benefit of all people.

Visions come in many forms and they may not be grand. Ms. Brian[1], for instance, was a plain nurse at a hospital. Whenever she was required to make a decision for her patient, she simply asked herself the question, "Am I doing everything I can for my patient?" Her patients consistently recovered more quickly than the rest of the patients in the hospital, and the hospital

---

1)   Drucker, Peter *op. cit.*

management eventually realized this and adopted her approach for the entire hospital.

Famous cyclist Lance Armstrong, winner of seven Tour de France championships, was an average competitor at the start of his racing career. After surviving from cancer, he resumed competing with a new purpose. He was determined to compete on behalf of all cancer patients to give them hope and courage. Armed with his new goal and mission, he was able to communicate better with his eight teammates and excelled in his races, achieving his record-breaking seven championships.

Peter Drucker, says that if one sets his sight on a mission for the good of the whole, he or she generates new energy. He feels comfortable communicating with others and finds like-minded people to build a team.

US Post Office in LA in memory of Dosan

Dosan Square in LA, USA

He helps himself and others as well.

Another important aspect in setting goals has to do with confidence and positive thinking. Confidence and positive thinking are two sides of the same coin, and it is always important to believe that "I'll be fine" and start fresh each and every day to move toward

Establish Meaning of Life. Dream and Set Goals

Dosan's Three Dreams
- Independence of the fatherland
- Strong Economy
- World's Respect for Koreans

- We live as happy as we want to. Likewise, a person with great ideals becomes a great person, and a person with mediocre ideals becomes a mediocre person.

- Set dreams, not for quick results but for the long-term common good.

- Confidence comes from positive thinking. Confidence and positive thinking are inextricably linked.

- Dosan's words on positive thinking and common good
  ① Some people will follow the truth for certain; justice will prevail someday for certain.
  ② Despair invites death to the youth; when the youth dies, the nation dies.
  ③ When I eat, I eat for the independence of Korea; when I sleep, I sleep for the independence of Korea.

the goal. One must not underestimate his or her own potential, nor should one become discouraged by criticisms or mistakes. One should learn from mistakes. If one focuses on positive thinking, things that were deemed impossible can be accomplished.

Dosan himself was an example of positive thinking. He comforted and encouraged those pessimists who thought achieving Korean independence was impossible. He never wavered from his belief that Japan would collapse because its imperialistic actions to colonize Korea were based on evil intent. His positive thinking made a solid foundation for his tenacious activities of the independence movement.

1.3 Leadership via Mu Shil (Pursuit of Truth)

Dosan strongly believed that honesty was the first step toward loving oneself. So he lived by the word Mu Shil, taught its concept to his students, and acted on it.

People follow a leader they trust. In order to gain peoples' trust, one must keep his promise; his words and actions must coincide; and he must be consistent. These qualities are not easily taught; and, one must acquire these on his own.

Kouzes and Posner conducted a study over a twenty-year period, in which they asked 75,000 people what they considered to be the top five characteristics for which they look in a leader. Honesty was the top answer. The table above summarizes the characteristics that people all across the globe selected.

Most of the renowned leaders throughout history held honesty and trust as their primary values. For

Characteristics of Admired Leaders (% of Respondents)

Character	Yr2007	Yr1987	Character	Yr2007	Yr1987
Honest	89	83	Courageous	25	27
Forward-looking	71	62	Cooperative	25	25
Inspiring	69	58	Determined	25	17
Competent	68	67	Caring	22	26
Intelligent	48	43	Imaginative	17	34
Fair-minded	39	40	Ambitious	16	21
Broad-minded	35	37	Mature	15	23
Straightforward	36	34	Loyal	18	11
Supportive	35	32	Self-controlled	10	13
Dependable	34	33	Independent	4	10

Source: Kouzes & Posner, *op. cit*

example, Mahatma Gandhi of India was known as a shy child, but he was remarkably honest. Once during an English test his teacher pointed out that he had written down a wrong answer on his test sheet and hinted that he should check for the right answer from the student next to him. Young Gandhi refused to look at his neighbor's test sheet, and the teacher told him afterwards that he was a fool for not consulting his neighbor. Gandhi replied, "I think it's wrong to look at someone else's test sheet." Needless to say, his honesty and determination were the foundation for his success in independence work later.

Mahatma (Great Spirit) Gandhi at his spinning wheel

When Dosan first arrived in San Francisco, he wanted to enter an elementary school to learn English and to have a firsthand experience in the American school system. However, he was refused because he was too old for elementary school. The age regulation only allowed students up to seventeen years old. His landlord suggested that he should tell them that he was seventeen instead of twenty-three because Dosan looked young. Dosan replied that he couldn't tell a lie,

Dosan recalls the time when he was kicked out of San Francisco school in 1902 because of his age

surprising the landlord. He tried other schools, and finally he was able to enter a school on his third try. The principal was impressed by Dosan's honesty and ambition. He invited Dosan to enter his school, saying, "The age limit only applies to American students, not foreign students."

John Zenger, a scholar and expert on the subject of corporate leadership, compares an organization to a tent. He points out that the leader's core "character" of honesty and trust is the center pole of the tent. Other

---

Leadership of Mu Shil: Pursuit of Truth

• Honesty is the most important element in leadership. Honesty generates trust among the members of his or her organization.

• Dosan's method in developing trustworthiness:
  ① Make meticulous plans based on accurate analysis of all the facts.
  ② Put forth the best effort and follow the plan until you achieve the mission. Do not compromise your principles.

• Dosan's words on Mu Shil leadership:
  ① Do not tell lies, even in death.
  ② Do not tell lies, even as a joke.
  ③ Exercise your contrition if you behaved in an insincere manner, even in your dreams.
  ④ Lies! You are the enemy that ruined my country.
  ⑤ Artificiality is the reason for defeat; conscientiousness is the foundation for success.

elements that form successful leadership are: individual ability, organizational skills, result-oriented approach, and concentration. These other elements form the peripheral poles of the tent. If any of them falter, the tent would remain standing due to the strength of the center pole. However, if the center pole — the "character" of the leader — falters, the tent collapses.

1.4 Developing Good Habits

Dosan believed that leaders were made, not born, and based his leadership development program on that premise. He emphasized cultivation and training coupled with the importance of good habits, as well as the hard work in developing them.

> "Beating an army of ten thousand is easy. But overcoming our habits is hard, and we must devote our lives to developing good habits."

The Greek philosopher Aristotle said, "We are

what we repeatedly do. Excellence, then, is not an act, but a habit." Horace Mann, the American educator, said, "Habit is a cable; we weave a thread of it every day, and at last we cannot break it."

Also, there is a variety of proverbs handed down from ancient times related to habits.

"Your thoughts become your words. Your words become your actions. Your actions become your habits. Your habits become your character. Your character becomes your destiny."

"We form our habits in the beginning, but our habits make us in the end."

Stephen Covey's view on habits is as follows:

"We define a habit as the intersection of knowledge, skill, and desire. Knowledge is the theoretical paradigm, the what to do and why. Skill is the how to do. And desire is the motivation, the want to do. In order to make something a habit in our lives, we have to have all three. Unless I search out correct principles of human interaction, I may not even know I need to listen. Even if I really need to listen to them, I may not have the skill. Unless I want to listen, unless I have the desire, it won't be a habit in my life."

Dale Carnegie, author of *How to Win Friends and Influence People*, points out the importance of developing the habit of maintaining good relations with people, i.e., remembering their names. Stephen Covey talks about developing a habit of doing important things first for the sake of efficient time management. Dosan, on the other hand, taught his students and followers that in addition to simple habits like being on time and keeping promises, they should develop habits to treat each other with honesty and affection in daily life.

Leadership by Training: Work Hard to Develop Good Habits

- Dosan truly believed that leaders are made, not born, and emphasized the need for the training to acquire and achieve leadership.

- Dosan's words with respect to good habits:
  ① Beating an army of ten thousand is easy. Overcoming our habits is hard, and we must devote our lives to developing good habits.
  ② Let us reform our mouths that are prone to lie and train them to tell only the truth.
  ③ Let us reform our lazy limbs and train them to become vibrant and diligent.

"I think one should strive to love every day and make that into a habit. Habits build one's character, creating virtue."

2
Loving Others: Ae Ta

Dosan's contemporary, Dale Carnegie, made the concept of winning friends and influencing people famous and became an expert in the field of leadership. Dosan Ahn Chang-Ho goes a step further and suggests the concept of "Ae Ta," love others the same way you love yourself. He may have based this leadership concept on the Christian teaching, "Love thy neighbor." Dosan became one of Korea's early converts to Christianity while he attended missionary school in Seoul.

The Ae Ta concept is an extension of Ae Ki, and it is just as demanding to manage and carry out.

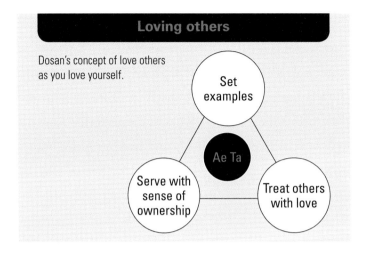

Earlier we discovered that Ae Ki requires constant training to attain sound mind, health, and knowledge. Ae Ta requires constant willingness to help others, thoughtfulness toward others, developing the sense of ownership, and treating others with love and affection.

2.1 Leadership by Setting Examples

A leader provides guidance for an organization. As a leader, he must show everyone how to perform their functions by doing the same functions himself. For instance, a president of a company who wants his employees to start work at eight in the morning must show up at eight o'clock himself in order to gain the trust of his employees. In Dosan's case, early Koreans in San Francisco were unruly and lived in filthy homes until young Dosan showed them the better way by cleaning their homes and planting flower beds outside. When they realized what Dosan was doing for them made sense, they believed in him and followed his lead. He taught them the importance of being honest and helpful to each other; consequently, the Korean community improved internally and externally. Koreans became more and more confident and positive in their outlook. An American landlord who realized Dosan was the person leading the change coined a phrase, "Dosan's Republic," referring to the development of the collective interests of the community.

Leadership by example often produces heroes at times of war. Despite his bad back, John F. Kennedy, 35th President of the United States, enlisted in the Navy during World War II. He served in the South Pacific as the commander of the PT-109 patrol boat, which sank after colliding with a Japanese destroyer. He rescued his crew, getting them safely onto the shore of a nearby island. Kennedy's bold leadership earned him the Navy and Marine Corps Medal and a Purple Heart medal. He maintained this style of leadership in his political life, first in the House of Representatives and then in the Senate, and eventually during his Presidency.

John McCain is another war hero who successfully transferred his style of leadership to the political arena. When he was a jet fighter pilot during the Vietnam War, he was shot down and captured. His

Dosan (third from left) with Korean farm laborers

captors found out that he was a son of a high ranking US Navy officer and the North Vietnamese offered to release him. However McCain refused to leave without his fellow airmen and spent five-and-a-half years in prison. His story was an inspiration to many, and helped him pursue his political career as a Congressman and Senator.

In setting examples, it is important for leaders to utilize their strengths. Researches show (e.g., Marcus Buckingham's book *Now, Discover Your Strengths*) that talented leaders have their weaknesses, too, but they are effective because their strengths are clearly defined and enriched. The list of strengths goes on and on, and anyone who utilizes his strengths can be an effective leader.

Another important aspect for a leader is his ability to speak in public. Dosan was a captivating speaker, and people gathered to hear him whenever and wherever he spoke. His first public speech was the "Quae Jae Jeong" speech in 1899 when he openly criticized the feudal leaders' political corruption, with many government officials in attendance. His passionate speech was delivered with so much sense and logic for a

Sign for Quae Jae Jeong, where Dosan's first speech took place.

young man of twenty years, the old government officials were rendered speechless despite his scathing criticisms about their corruption and usurping of power. The audience was ecstatic because he vocalized all the things they were thinking, while they were bound by cultural traditions to remain silent about their own thoughts.

Park Jae-hoo was in the audience and recalled his experience in the September issue of "*Sae Byok* (Dawn)" magazine in 1954.

> "Ahn Chang-Ho is a heroic marvelous speaker. The Governor and the Constable were tongue-tied and kept their heads down the whole time Dosan spoke. People, young and old, hung on to every word he said. He is in America now, and when he comes back, he will do great things [for our country]."

He made countless speeches while he was in America, founding several organizations in the process and continued to make speeches when he went back to Korea in 1907. Jang Ri-wook, Dosan's disciple and a highly accomplished member of the Hungsadan, compared Dosan's speaking ability with Abraham Lincoln's speech skills. Dosan didn't leave behind a tremendous volume of writing, but, like those of Lincoln, his writings impressed his contemporaries tremendously and continue to resonate with people today, seventy plus years after his death.

Lincoln's Gettysburg Address and the Emancipation Proclamation define his moment in

A crowd gathering for Dosan's speech

history, and so do Dosan's speeches and his "Words to My Countrymen." Dosan's speeches were more like lectures given in plain language with a lot of examples. Yi Kwang-su describes Dosan's voice as "deep and gentle, neither loud nor soft and with a tinge of sadness." Jang Ri-wook adds, "Dosan's speeches are characterized by his meticulous preparation, clear message, ample quotes by other people, and his use of plain language yet very creative." In short, Dosan was a born orator with God-given talents and penchant for research and meticulous preparation. He provides us with a perfect example of utilizing one's strength.

Dosan also had a good habit of listening to others. Yi Kwang-su writes: "Dosan listened to people with keen interest, never interrupting anyone in the middle of a speech. He listened to every word, and when the speaker finished, he would ask questions to confirm the details."

Dosan's biographers, Yi Kwang-su, Chu Yohan, and Jang Ri-wook, describe Dosan as a rational intellectual, pointing out the superior logic contained in his speeches and writings. We can appreciate his logic in his Master Plan for the Independence Movement

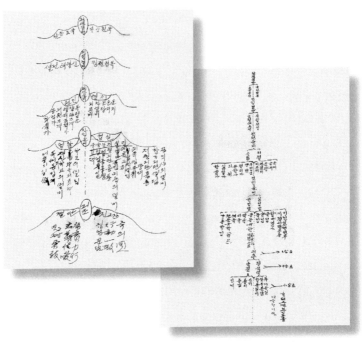

Dosan's strategy for the independence movement (1913)

that he devised in 1913.

He provided the crucial logic in formulating the basic strategy at every major turning point of the Korean independence movement. He led the formation of Shin Min Hoe, the secret society composed of all the key historical figures in the Korean independence movement. He organized the Korean National Association and the Hungsadan in America. And in

Shanghai, he was the main organizer of the Provisional Government of Korea. According to Chu Yohan, "When a discussion arose among the comrades with respect to the direction and strategy for the independence movement, they always adopted Dosan's views in the end. Sometimes, this became cause for jealousy by other participants who conspired against him."

Jang Ri-wook writes, "He possessed an intellect of a higher level." Dosan's morals and lofty character make him an extraordinary man, considering the fact that he had no scandal of any kind, which is rare among personalities of his political stature. Jang suggests that the combination of his high morals and rational intellect played a very important role in the independence movement.

Finally, Jang points to Dosan's big heart for humanity. He treated everyone with genuine love and respect and had an uncanny ability, a sixth sense perhaps, of knowing what people were thinking. He was a humanist from beginning to the end, and he based all his actions on his humanistic view on life. His incessant call for a "community filled with affection" and "fellowship" comes from that humanistic point of view.

In summary, Dosan utilized his strengths — oratory talent, logical thinking, sound morals, and humanism — to the fullest as he provided his leadership for the independence movement. That is the reason why he continues to receive love and respect today.

But Dosan was not without weaknesses. He hailed from the Northwest region of the Korean peninsula, an area that was largely neglected and discriminated against. He also came from a humble background, born on a poor farm and not of the *yangban* (noble) class. He lacked academic credentials. These negatives truly worked against him in the political arena. Therefore, he strived to practice humility. As the main organizer of the Korean Provisional Government, Dosan himself took a lower post and supported Syngman Rhee for the top post because Rhee's *yangban* class background with a Ph.D. from Princeton University boded well for representing Korea. Rhee had many opponents. However, Dosan worked hard to persuade his colleagues of the value of Rhee's qualifications.

Dosan had another weakness: his smoking habit.

Dosan's tobacco pipes

He tried hard to quit smoking, but he couldn't. In conclusion, Dosan had his weaknesses, too, but he persevered to maximize his strengths and utilized them to the fullest, which made him the premier leader of the time.

In addition, a leader must be capable of recognizing strengths in his subordinates or members of his organization and utilizing their strengths for the good of the whole. There is a famous story about Abraham Lincoln and the commanding general of the

Union Army, Ulysses S. Grant. Grant was a notorious drinker, and people criticized him for it. Responding to the criticism, Lincoln asked what brand of whisky Grant preferred, so he could send the same brand to the rest of his generals. As a youngster growing up in

Leadership by Yeok Hang: Set Examples

- A leader guides an organization. If the leader himself does not carry out what he wants his members to do, no one will follow him or her.

- What's important in carrying out your mission is to maximize your strengths. All leaders have weaknesses. An outstanding leader is one who clearly possesses strengths and utilizes them effectively.

Dosan's Strengths	- Oratory skills and reasonableness - Lofty character and warm heart - Capability to carry out actions
Dosan's Weaknesses	- Born poor in Pyong An Province - Lack of formal schooling - Smoking habit

- Dosan's words on Yeok Hang
  ① I do my utmost to accomplish my mission for today.
  ② You, me, all of us—let us become the people of action.
  ③ I try to complete today all the tasks I was supposed to do today.
  ④ Do you love your country? Then you become a wholesome character first.
  ⑤ If you feel the pain of the people, then you become a doctor.

Kentucky, Lincoln had seen the harmful effect alcohol had on people, yet he was willing to send his generals whatever Grant was drinking. In appointing Grant as the commander, Lincoln was thinking about Grant's winning record on battlefields, not his weakness of being a drinker. If Lincoln looked for a general without any weakness, a sober general for instance, he would not have appointed Grant for the job and would not have won the war.

Marcus Buckingham, a management expert who developed a program related to self-discovery of personal strengths, suggests distinguishing indigenous talents from acquired skills through learning. Discovering one's inherent strengths helps one plan his life accordingly and enhances his chance for success. If a leader of an organization discovers the strengths of his employees and utilizes them accordingly, the employees would be happier performing their duties.

2.2 Sense of Ownership (Proprietorship)

Sense of ownership is one of the crucial elements in Dosan's leadership model. Dosan's sense of ownership means sense of responsibility, and sense of responsibility leads to service and sacrifice for the whole organization. The concept of "servant leadership" was first introduced by Robert Greenleaf in the early 1970s. Traditionally, a servant serves a master under trying circumstances, and not out of voluntary devotion. On the other hand, a master of a home (proprietor, owner) serves his guest with respect and kindness because he feels responsible for the guest and his comfort. That is the spirit of the servant leadership that Dosan practiced and taught.

> "Those who feel responsible for the nation's well-being are proprietors, those who do not feel the responsibility for the nation are visitors."

When the owner of a home invites a guest, he does everything he can to entertain his guest with food, drinks, and other creature comforts. When some problem occurs, he gets right into it and tries to solve the problem. This is the basic principle of "servant leadership." On the other hand, if the owner ignores the guest's wishes and thoughts and imposes his will on his guest, the guest will be displeased, wishing to leave the house.

The reason the owner serves the guest is not because the guest is higher in stature, but because it is the proper thing to do as an owner. Accordingly, a leader in a democratic society does not issue commands for the people to follow blindly, but understands the people and their desires.

In conclusion, an owner serves a guest out of his sense of responsibility. But the guest does not feel the sense of responsibility because he expects to be served.

Greenleaf's servant leadership, then, can be better explained by Dosan's concept of ownership. Greenleaf says that the idea of "servant leadership" came to him after reading Herman Hesse's book, *Journey to the East*, a novel about a group of travelers (the League) who set out for a mystical pilgrimage to the East in search of the ultimate truth. Protagonist Leo joins the journey as a servant to take care of chores, but when the group falls into difficulties, he sings songs to rejuvenate them.

Mother Teresa

The journey is fun and smooth until Leo disappears. The group becomes confused and gives up on the trip because they couldn't continue without Leo the servant. It turns out that Leo was not just a simple servant. The narrator of the story, H.H., eventually tracks Leo down only to learn that Leo was not a servant but in reality he was the head of the League, which sponsored the journey.

Mother Teresa is a prime example of servant leadership. Born in Macedonia in 1910, she decided to become a nun when she was twelve years old. She began

Leadership by Service: Serve with a Sense of Ownership

- Greenleaf obtained the idea of servant leadership by reading Herman Hesse's book, Journey to the East. The novel's main character, Leo, was a servant, yet he was the owner of the organization that sponsored the journey. He started out as the humble servant for the group and he became the actual leader of the group.

- To Dosan, the sense of ownership meant responsibility to serve and sacrifice oneself for the benefit of the entire organization.

- Dosan's words on ownership:
  ① In the nation's society, people with the sense of responsibility are the owners; if not, they are just guests.
  ② True owners of our nation hold neither positive nor negative views. They only feel responsible to find ways to save our nation.
  ③ In every household, if there is no owner, the house falls down or some stranger takes over. The same goes for a nation and society.
  ④ A hero is no one special. Anyone who works with a heart of a hero is a hero.

her life as a nun in Calcutta, India, helping feed the poor people there. Her role model was Saint Therese of Lisieux, who believed that one must forfeit oneself in order to follow a spiritual path. In 1950, Mother Teresa founded the Missionaries of Charity along with twelve supporters. She said, "We ourselves feel that what we are doing is just a drop in the ocean. But the ocean would be less because of that missing drop." Mother Teresa's small act for the poor and the sick grew to become the largest service organization in the world. Her spirit of service is the key to its continued success.

2.3 Love and Fellowship

People are moved by love, the most powerful force known to mankind. Love is said to melt the snow that was built up over ten thousand years and love moves mountains. Man is an emotional being, and love is at the center of all human emotions. It is only natural that a leader should embrace and love people.

Kouzes & Posner talk about love as the main ingredient for leadership:

> "After numerous interviews and case analyses, we were struck by how many leaders used the word "love" freely when talking about their own motivation to lead, in explaining why they endured the hardships, made the personal sacrifices, and accomplished what

they did. Of all the things that sustain a leader over time, love is the longest lasting. It is hard to imagine leaders without having their hearts in it getting up day after day, and putting in the long hours and hard work it takes to get extraordinary things done. This may just be the best kept secret of successful leaders. If you love what you're doing, you will never have to work. Stay in love with leading, stay in love with the people who do the work. Leadership is not an affair of the head. Leadership is an affair of the heart."

Dosan recognized the importance of love and created the concept of Ae Ki Ae Ta. Rhonda Byrne[2] says "We have nothing to give to others if we do not satisfy our own quest for love. Love of others begins with love of ourselves. Doing what you love translates to happiness, and your enthusiasm spills over to others."

The love theory works on animals like killer whales. As big as they are, weighing over four tons, they respond to praise and affection when they are trained for shows. The whale's trainer begins by feeding them and swimming with them to earn their trust. And when the whale follows the trainer's instructions, the trainer

---

2) Byrne, Rhond, *op. cit.*

Dolphin and killer whale

strokes the whale's head, praising it and strengthening its trust. Amazingly, praising whales is much more effective than feeding them. Also, it is difficult to punish whales when they do something wrong. So when the whales make mistakes, the trainer leaves them alone and lets them rest for a long time, after which the whales apply themselves harder for more praises. This method can be applied to employees or children at home.

Dosan considered that the biggest problem with the Korean society at the time was lack of love. Lack of love was the main cause of the society's divisiveness, and he exhorted Koreans to practice love among fellow countrymen and unite together.

"Unity is not a product of idealism, but of love."

Many people allude to the importance of love, but only a few suggest how to practice it. Dosan had his own ideas about how to practice love. First, Dosan believed that love could be attained through practice, just as one could train oneself to develop good habits such as being on time. Similarly, he believed that one could practice fellowship among the members of an organization to foster an affectionate relationship like the one between parents and their children. He believed and taught his colleagues that practicing love and fellowship began with respect and trust of others as individuals.

Leadership by Fellowship: Love Is the Key Ingredient

- People are moved by love, the most powerful force known to mankind. Man is an emotional being, and love is at the center of all human emotions. Love can change people.

- Dosan's explanation on fellowship:
  ① Fellowship means putting our ceaseless effort into practicing love.
  ② The feeling of affection associated with fellowship is similar to mother's love for her child, as well as her willingness to share her child's pleasures and pains.

- Dosan's words on love
  ① Why is our society so cold? There is no warmth. We should love each other and build a society filled with smiles.
  ② Let us study about love, you and I. I ask our twenty million men and women to become one loving people.
  ③ Ideology does not hold a group together. Love does.
  ④ There is often water under a dried-up spring. You will find the water if you dig a little. If you do not find the water, then dig deeper. This is how you study about love. You can grow love in your heart by studying about love.

3
Love of Organization: Patriotism

What does it mean to love the organization that you are serving? For Dosan, his organization meant his country, and his love was expressed in terms of patriotism. Once he told his Japanese jailer, "My job is independence work. I eat and sleep for independence of my fatherland." This phrase is similar to a phrase in the Bible, Corinthians Chapter 10, verse 31, "Whether therefore ye eat, or drink, or whatsoever ye do, do all to the glory of God."

Dosan was very serious about his independence work, which was indeed the "purpose of his life," even comparing his passion to Christians' faith. We can break down his patriotism into three areas: leadership for transformation, democratic leadership, and leadership for unity.

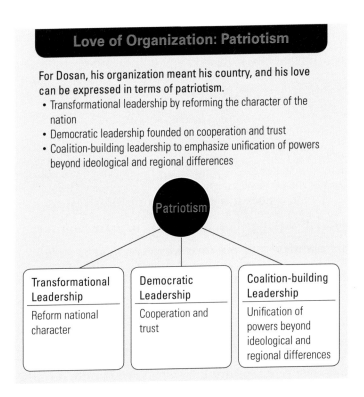

3.1 Leading the Reform

The twenty-first century is a century of change, marked by the changes in technology as fast as the speed of thoughts, not to mention the changes in the environment we live in. It behooves us to recognize and analyze the changing times and reflect these changes in the organization to which we belong. Nobody in the world can tell us what is important for us. When we fall down, we have to figure out why we fell and then find the way to get up on our own. Likewise, we have to strive to reform on our own, utilizing our creativity to adapt to new ways. The need-to-change impacts every aspect of our lives, including our body, spirit, emotion, and soul. Each of these areas requires specific methods to deal with them.

Reforming an organization requires a leader with ability to think creatively as well as having the capability to execute the changes its members desire. The leader must possess the will to propel the organization's agenda, form new visions, and encourage the members of the organization to support the changes.

Jack Welch, the chairman of General Electric,

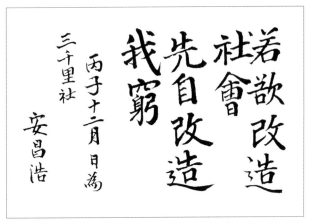

Dosan's calligraphy on reform(1936)

was an outstanding transformational leader. Taking over the top post in 1981, he saw that GE was not changing with the times, losing its market share in electronic products around the world. In turning around the struggling company, he devised a slogan, "Be the first or second" and gave up on marginal products and their related departments. His three main philosophies in adapting to the changing world were "change before it's too late," "look straight at the reality, don't avoid it," and "slim down the organization before it's too late."

Computer giant IBM was struggling during the mid-1990s, when new CEO Louis Gerstner came on the scene. He transformed the organizational culture from producer-centric to a customer service base, staving off the crisis situation. He streamlined the stale, cumbersome structure that often bogged down. His leadership and vision turned IBM into an organization that was sensitive to the changes that customers wanted.

Ahn Chol-su is another successful CEO who subscribed to reform philosophy. Ahn is a medical doctor who became interested in developing a vaccine against computer viruses. He studied medicine and computer science together over a seven-year period and founded the Ahn Chol-su Research Center in 1995, focusing on fixing computer ailments. Thus he successfully transformed himself from a medical doctor to a computer doctor. He continues to use his creative leadership as CEO to search for new ideas that reflect the changing times.

Dosan realized the need to change the environment for his countrymen a century ago; and that the responsibility rested with individuals to do their part to change in order to recover the loss of Korea to Japan. He stressed the need for a new paradigm, to purge the atmosphere of deceit and falsehood and build a new enlightened society based on truth, love, and unity.

"Well cared for pear trees bear high quality pears
and wild pear trees bear shabby pears. As such, a
nation of people that is qualified to live independently
deserves the fruits of independence. Conversely, for a
nation that is only qualified to live under oppression,
the fruits of bankruptcy await them."

"If we are to reform the nation, we need to reform
each one of us individually. No one else can make
us achieve transformation; each of us must reform
ourselves as individuals."

Dosan's idea of reform is unique in that he doesn't
stop at the character development of individuals. He
extends his goal to include issues related to economics
and all of the elements that make up our society. He
argues that we must reform our religion, education,
agriculture, and commerce.

"If you love our nation as I do, then let us endeavor
together, you and I, and reform our nation. Let
us reform our education, religion, agriculture,
commerce, construction, our traditions and habits.
Food, clothes, homes. Our cities and farms. And even

our rivers and mountains."

Warren Bennis, an expert in the leadership field, defines a transformational leader as someone who can inspire people to act, someone who can transform followers to leaders, and someone who can make them agents of change. Bennis adds other elements to the list, such as charisma to motivate members of his organization, ability to motivate his subordinates to search for new solutions to problems, and ability to encourage his subordinates.

Dosan Ahn Chang-Ho fits Bennis' definition of a transformational leader, and we can see evidence of this leadership in the Hungsadan organization. Dosan had founded the Hungsadan to develop future leaders to carry out independence work for Korea. He inspired the Hungsadan members to seek truths and act on them in his speeches and by setting examples of them. He motivated them to find new solutions to their problems and encouraged them to implement these solutions in their lives.

He was a true transformational leader. He reformed himself by acquiring new information about the world around him and acted accordingly to implement the necessary changes. He constantly searched for new creative solutions to society's problems and communicated the new changes to his colleagues. He let the new ideas flow freely to plant the seed of reform.

Creativity is the prime mover for many successful endeavors. Born in 1901, Walt Disney utilized his creativity for his mission "to make people happy" and built his organization as one of the top leaders in the entertainment industry. He made history in the field of entertainment by creating characters like Mickey Mouse and Donald Duck, as well as receiving forty-eight Academy Awards and seven Emmys. He died in 1966, but his successful enterprise still goes on with ten theme parks, dozens of hotels, a movie studio, and a cable TV network.

Bill Gates is another leader who successfully put his creativity to good use. He began computer programming at age thirteen and founded Microsoft in 1975 to develop the operating software for personal computers. Today, he works hard to maintain his position as the number one software provider in the world, always searching for new ideas and turning them into new enterprises. He believes that he should create a company as big as Coca-Cola every five years and that the speed of operating businesses must be as quick as forming thoughts.

Creativity in the field of IT (Information Technology) continues to be the prime factor in generating new businesses. Stanford graduate students Larry Page and Sergey Brin developed a new web search engine and founded Google, which grew into the top internet-based service company within ten years. Steve Jobs overcame his difficulties of losing Apple, the company he founded, liver cancer, and successfully created new items such as the iPod, iPhone, and iPad.

The Samsung Company is also a good example of creative management. Faced with a currency crisis in 1997, the CEO of Samsung Lee Gun-hee proposed to "change everything except our wives" in a daring move to reform its product line. As the result,

Steve Jobs

Samsung surpassed Sony as one of the top electronics firm in the world. Facing the global financial crisis in 2008, he insisted on maintaining costly branches around the world instead of closing them. Samsung has changed its reporting structure, from a ladder-type to round table discussion. Samsung is now a leading company in chip manufacturing, LCD, telephones, and digital media.

During the days of the independence movement, the majority of independence workers believed that resistance should be the foundation for all of the independence activities. Dosan believed in resistance and military action against Imperial Japan, but he also believed in building the internal strength of the Korean people. The lack of strength was responsible for losing the country in the first place, and he instituted the concept of "building strength" as the basic philosophy for the independence movement. For Dosan, strength meant three things: one, a strong army to fight the independence war; two, economic strength; and three, global respect. Dosan was interested in cultivating leaders in the economic sector as well, in addition to the fields of politics and education. He founded corporate entities with stockholders, pioneering the way for Korean corporations.

There have been a number of outstanding leaders throughout Korean history. Born in 1397, King Sejong was a man of many talents. He was responsible for creating the Korean alphabet, inventing the water clock, a sundial,

King Sejong and linguists creating Korean alphabets

and a rain gauge. He is regarded as the people's king for his approach to his crown as "a tool for the people" and for his penchant for listening to his subordinates and the common man. He was open to different ideas and endeavored to improve the quality of life for the common folk, including education, which at that time was limited to the upper class. He was an avid reader, well informed in science, literature, and culture, which helped him generate new ideas and lead discussions with his subordinates.

Admiral Yi Soon-shin was born into a family

Admiral Yi Soon-shin's calligraphy for his troops

of scholars. He liked shooting the bow and arrow as a child, and became a military man who later repelled Japanese invaders, winning all of his twenty-three battles against them. Besides his naval acumen, he was a man of high morals as well as a capable leader, and he is revered by all Koreans as a heroic historical figure.

His leadership philosophy is expressed in his calligraphy, "PIL SA JEUK SANG, PIL SANG JEUK SA," meaning, "Be prepared to die, then you will live. Be afraid of dying, then you will die." He spoke these words the day before the battle of MyungRahng, in which he destroyed hundreds of enemy ships with his mere twelve ships. His victory was possible because of his uniquely designed turtle ships and his superior strategy, not to mention his will to persevere. His meticulous battle plan had a lot to do with his winning strategy. He studied the MyungRahng strait in detail and practiced luring enemy ships into the narrow channel. As he led the battle, his flagship took the front and kept his position despite the fierce enemy attack, inspiring the rest of his fleet to carry out the battle plan

Transformational Leadership: Provides Guidance for Changes

- The 21st century is the era of change. Accordingly, a leader must be able to provide guidance for his organization in this changing world by creative means.

- Resistance against Imperial Japan was the main thrust for Dosan's contemporaries. Dosan believed that they should first treat the fundamental problem that was responsible for Korea's demise.

- Dosan established his basic philosophy of "building strength" and focused on cultivating manpower.

- In addition to his political and educational endeavors, Dosan formed Korea's first corporation.

- Dosan's words on reformation
  ① I regard human beings as animals that engage in transformation.
  ② If you love our country and I love our country, let us join our forces to reform our country.
  ③ If we are to reform all the people of Korea, we must first reform each individual. Each individual should reform himself or herself. No one else can do it for them.
  ④ There is only one way for Korea to produce leaders. It is up to each one of us to commit ourselves to study and train to become leaders.

to success.

King Sejong's creative leadership, Admiral Yi's victories over the Japanese armada with his famed turtle ships, and Dosan's vision for modernizing Korea make for some of the bright spots in Korean history.

3.2 Democratic Leadership: Sharing Together

There is an old Korean adage, "A piece of paper carried by two makes it even lighter," meaning that you can make a simple task even easier by sharing the burden. "Two heads are better than one" is another way to express the concept. We now live in an information age. Information is at the heart of all activities, individual or group. Information is power, and when you combine one set of information with another, it is doubly powerful. For example, when we combine information technology with biotech, we are able to delve deeper into the mystery of hereditary genes. Accordingly, experts in different fields working together can achieve great things, and a good leader should know how to organize and facilitate the experts' activities.

Sharing information is a prerequisite for leaders in a democratic society. George Washington was made the commanding general for the colonial army in June 1775, and he focused on bringing together the rag-tag American colonists from thirteen states in preparation for the independence war against the British Empire's mighty military machine. He is known for his democratic leadership, always discussing plans and strategies with his commanders. He had high respect for their opinions and utilized their talents effectively. He was receptive to opposing views and a master in building consensus. Likewise, he commanded respect from his colleagues and subordinates, and they elected him the first President of the United States. As President, he succeeded in consolidating a variety of people and ideas from thirteen states, serving in the office of Presidency for two terms. His famous quote, "A dictatorial style, though it may carry conviction, is always accompanied with disgust," expresses his philosophy as the democratic leader, setting the foundation for the young, independent republic.

King Sejong also was known for his ability to build consensus among his subordinates at a time when absolute obedience to the crown was the order of the day. As the newly crowned twenty-three-year old, his first words to his court were "I need your help with the formation of my new cabinet. I will make my decision after ample discussion with you." Subsequently, he held open, candid discussions with his subordinates whenever problems arose. He encouraged them to speak their minds, turning the otherwise oppressive royal court into a comfortable study group. Open minded, he was receptive to opposing views as well, and no task was untouchable. He was able to build consensus on difficult projects like the Korean alphabets, defense issues, and diplomacy.

Dosan's biographer Chu Yohan called Dosan the "model democratic leader." Dosan acquired his democratic vision while he lived America for a number of years, notably in Riverside, California, at a time when the area was burgeoning as a center of the citrus industry. There, he was a laborer, labor organizer, educator, and labor negotiator, putting him in the middle of democracy at work at the grass roots level. We can get a glimpse of his democratic principles through his speeches to the Hungsadan members and writings in *Dong Gwang* magazine during the early 1900s. First, he points out we must recognize that each of us has a unique personality as an individual, and we should respect that.

"Square rock or rounded boulder, each of them has its own use, and we should not rebuke those whose personalities are different from mine."

"If I am right about something, we should recognize the fact that others may be right as well. We will enjoy peace and harmony if we stop despising those with different opinions."

"We must, as cultural beings, recognize the freedom of thought and speech of each other, and always maintain fellowship and respect even though we may differ in our views."

According to Yi Kwang-su, "Dosan was never interested in matters related to people's private lives. He ignored any rumors or gossiping altogether." His respect for individual rights and equality was exemplary. During his interviews with prospective Hungsadan

Dosan with the Hungsadan members

members, Dosan always spoke to them in equal terms, even with seventeen-year-olds, demonstrating his attitude toward social equality.

Dosan was very impressed by the cordial fellowship between Democrats and Republicans in the aftermath of a fierce battle during a presidential election. Once the election was over, everyone respected the President and got behind him.

The spirit of cooperation is founded on trust. The culture of trust begins with one party opening up himself or herself to another and sharing information and resources, and that party must be "me." In order to foster the culture of trust we must determine the goal for the cooperating parties and decide the roles each party plays in order to achieve the goal.

In founding and organizing the Hungsadan, Dosan carried out the democratic leadership. He trusted everyone who passed the rigorous interview process that he designed. He instituted various group activities for the members to get together and trust each other. They frequently dined together and engaged in sporting events and played in a musical band together. He used his logic and conversational skills and facilitated meaningful discourse among the members. During the process the members formed a common sense of mission according to Dosan's vision for independence and reform. All the while, he was developing their leadership skills, by showing them that a leader did not think and plan everything himself, but reinforced the members' capability to make sound decisions. Enhancing their ability to make sound decisions meant "education, education, and more education" for the members. To that end, he turned himself into a coach, not one to only bark out commands. He focused on "empowering" the membership a long time before it became a common tool in practicing democratic leadership.

Dosan was a proponent of "one skill, one expertise" for everyone to master and fulfill his or her role as a productive contributor to the organization. He lamented the fact that the society at the time had a bad habit of looking down on productive activity due to the influence of Confucian tradition. In arguing against

Democratic Leadership: Sharing Together

- There is a saying, "If you want to go fast, go alone. If you want to go the distance, go together." Learning to share together is important for a leader.

- Chu Yohan referred to Dosan as the "model for a democratic leader," a rarity in modern Korean history.

- Dosan's words on democratic leadership:
  ① Square rock or rounded boulder, each of them has its own use, and we should not rebuke those with personalities that are different from one's own.
  ② If I am right about something, we should recognize the fact that others may be right as well. We will enjoy peace and harmony if we stop despising those with different opinions.
  ③ We must recognize the freedom of speech and thought between each other, and always maintain fellowship and respect, even though we may differ in our views.
  ④ We are free people, never to be subjected to slavery. We should only accept commands that arise from our conscience and ideals.

such attitude, he pointed to himself as an expert in cleaning homes. People of the *yangban* class (nobility) did not engage in physical labor of any sort. They did not lift or carry anything, never rushing anywhere. Dosan urged that productive physical activity even for politicians and artists was important in building a wholesome society.

3.3 Uniting Goals: Leadership by Building Consensus

Synergy is a phenomenon that occurs when a group of people rally around a common cause. It sometimes defies logic, and the leader must develop the skills to maintain the energy of the group and lead them to achieve their goals. This requires recognition of differences among individuals and keeping their teamwork going at the same time. It also is important to listen to everyone's opinions and maintain the atmosphere that encourages the search of new and improved solutions for the group.

People are ready to devote themselves to a leader who recognizes their talents and encourages them. When the leader recognizes the contributions the members make and rewards them, they will do their best. This is possible when the leader gets close to the members and utilizes the strengths each member possesses as well as providing them with incentives.

Sir Winston Churchill was a leader with unusual ability to unite people during WWII with his memorable comments, such as, "Courage is what it takes to stand up and speak; courage is also what it takes to sit down and listen." He inspired Britons to "Never give in — never, never, never, never, in nothing great or small, large or petty, never give in except to convictions of honor and good sense" and "I have nothing to offer but blood, toil, tears, and sweat." As Prime Minister during the worst crisis Britain ever faced, he led

Dosans's calligraphy on cooperation (1934)

the Britons to withstand the endless bombing by Nazi Germany and kept them going to victory over Hitler's military machine.

Dosan, as it was mentioned earlier, was a remarkable orator and he was able to persuade Korean laborers and farmers living in America to donate 10 to 25% of their income for independence work and to finance the founding of the Korean Provisional Government in Shanghai.

He felt that the sorely lacking sense of unity among his fellow countrymen was a major problem. He strived to bring them together by advancing new ideas for building solidarity based on common ground. He continually emphasized unity for those who were divided along ideological lines, Yi Dong-hwi on the left and Syngman Rhee on the right. "Unity is far more important than ideology in our struggle against Imperial Japan." He pointed to jealousy as the prime reason for their pejorative stance against each other and urged the two groups to develop mutual respect for each other.

"What is the reason for the disconnect everywhere?

It is not the petty provincialism, nor is it based on political preference. It is because of a few individuals' reluctance to subjugate themselves to each other."

"Our unity should not be based on our emotion. Our unity is our task as one nation…. We cannot truly unite without mutual trust, it doesn't matter that we share the same policy. Without trust it would be impossible to set common goals and methods."

From 1919 to 1932, Dosan devoted all his energy to uniting all the forces participating in the independence movement. He continued his effort to bring together feuding parties, Syngman Rhee on the right and Yi Dong-hwi on the left even after he resigned his cabinet position. Dosan facilitated the convention of all the representatives and founded the Great Independence Party in order to unite all the divisive factions. However, he was not able to achieve his dream despite all of his effort, which indicates how serious the division was at the time. The divisiveness continued even after independence came with the liberation from Japan at the end of World War II in 1945. The euphoria of liberation was short-lived, however, as the

Rowing   Rafting

division expanded to the general public and into a full-scale confrontation. The catastrophic Korean War followed and the divisiveness persists today between North Korea and South Korea. The inability to build any sort of consensus is an indication of the lack of true leadership.

Another important aspect in leadership is "alignment of goals in the same direction" allowing the organization to devise appropriate strategies to achieve those goals. Let us compare rowing and rafting to illustrate this point. A rowing team works in unison toward the finish line as directed by its leader according to the game plan. Each member of the team performs his given role assigned by the leader. The team leader and the members are required to cooperate in a steady situation. Rafting is similar to rowing in that this water sport also requires teamwork and cooperation in order to achieve the common goal. What is different is the environment in which the team has to work. In rafting, the conditions of the water vary in a quick fashion from one second to another and the team leader and the members must make fast adjustments accordingly. It tests the team's spontaneity and ability to react quickly.

Dosan points out the importance of the ability to analyze situations in an objective, deliberate manner in order to come up with an effective strategy to achieve the organization's goals.

> "In order to come up with ideas for unity, you and I need to maintain our cool heads wherever we are, deep in our own rooms, in the mountain, or meadow, we must do our due diligence in searching for the right plans and methods."

Dosan also points out that if Koreans share their love for their fatherland, they could unite their efforts toward this common goal despite their differences. An orchestra, for instance, is comprised of musicians playing a myriad instruments, each focused on his or her particular sound toward the common goal of

Leadership by Coalition: Building Consensus

- Synergy is a phenomenon that occurs when a group of people rally around a common cause.

- One important aspect of building consensus is the alignment of goals in the same direction.

- Dosan devoted all his energy to uniting all the forces. He emphasized that unity came before ideology.

- Dosan's words on unity:
  ① If we unite, we will prosper. Divided, we will fail. If we unite, we will live. Divided, we will die.
  ② We Koreans may have different ideas, but if we all love our country as one people, we can find success through that common goal.
  ③ We need to build our solidarity today, not based on our emotions but with a vision for our nation.
  ④ Let us faithfully devote all our energy to research the ways for building our unity and make plans accordingly.

producing music in harmony. Love for fatherland is the harmony Dosan sought in bringing together the various factions.

"Despite the endless opinions and thoughts that pitted us against each other, we can unite ourselves through our friendship and patriotism. Then, ideological confrontation can serve as a stimulus for discussions and training ground for advancing our cause. Mutual respect and affection will serve as a rope to bind us together as one, no matter how different our views are in terms of the fate of our nation."

Characteristics of Ae Ki Ae Ta Leadership

Dosan taking a picture of laborers and their families, circa 1912

1
Love Makes Everything Grow

Thus far, we have surveyed the ten principles that make up Dosan's leadership philosophy. Mu Shil Yeok Hang is best known in Korea as the foundation for the Hungsadan. Dosan's proprietorship concept also is well known among Korean students and the public because of its inclusion in text books. Of all of them, however, love is the most essential element in Dosan's leadership. Dosan related love to his colleagues as a form of fellowship. The word "fellowship" was one of Dosan's favorite words according to his biographers Yi Kwang-su and Chu Yohan.

Yi Kwang-su quoted Dosan in his biography on

the subject of love as following:

> "A couple's happiness depends on the love they
> have for each other. Prosperity for an organization
> and for a nation depends on the love and affection
> its members have for each other. Love for humanity
> enhances world peace and harmony. Confucius taught
> us about benevolence. Buddha taught us about mercy,
> and Jesus taught us about love. It is remarkable that
> all three of them shared similar thoughts for the good
> of humanity. Love is the righteous path for mankind."

> "An organization without respect for truth is like a
> body without blood, or a brick fence without mortar.
> An organization without sympathy and love for its
> principles, its members, and its leaders will eventually
> fail no matter how rich and strong it is today."

Chu Yohan, another biographer of Dosan, recorded what Dosan's colleagues said:

> "I think Dosan's ideas of love and devotion can only
> be matched by Jesus himself."

Dosan left behind three key illustrations of his calligraphy — "Ae Ki Ae Ta, Hyup Tong (Cooperation),

Yak Yok Gae Jo Sa Hoi, Sun Ja Gae Ah Goong (one must reform oneself before he can reform society). He wrote these pieces during the final stages of his life. His second calligraphy "Hyup Tong" was produced in April 1934, and his third one in December 1936. Ae Ki Ae Ta does not have a date on it. These three calligraphy pieces clearly represent his philosophy in life, especially Ae Ki Ae Ta.

The main theme for Ae Ki Ae Ta is love. Dosan became a Christian when he entered the Miller Academy in Seoul as a seventeen-year-old and was exposed to the Western concept of love. As an eager student of the Bible, he was convinced that without a doubt faith and good deeds are born out of love.

Yi Kwang-su writes that a Chinese physiognomist, after seeing Dosan's facial features, once told him that "Dosan was too kind to become a cruel revolutionary or politician." Dosan occasionally preached in churches, but religion was not a be-all-end-all ultimate proposition for him. However, he gravitated toward the concept of love out of his exposure to Christianity by missionaries in Seoul and his experiences while living in America.

Dr. Martin Luther King, Jr. was a man who truly loved humanity, the reason why so many people respect and honor him.

> "Anyone can be great... because anyone can serve. You don't have to have a college degree to serve. You don't have to make your subject and verb agree to serve. You only need a heart full of grace. A soul generated by love."

Cardinal Kim Su-hwan, whom Koreans selected as one of their most respected men in recent times, said that he admired Dosan the most of all historical figures.

Cardinal Kim Su-hwan

He believed that the ends did not justify the means just as Dosan had believed.

"Dosan Ahn Chang-Ho teaches us, 'There are those who follow the truth, and for them justice eventually will triumph. Swear with your life that you will always tell the truth.' These are words that we should carve in our hearts and minds. Dosan Ahn Chang-Ho's independence work was very valuable. The reason I came to respect him more was inspired by his philosophy. He always exhorted that we should pursue independence and self-respect by choosing a truthful way of life. There was no one like him among the independence movement leaders."

Pi Chun-deuk, most admired for his poetic essays, wrote:

"Two things impressed me as genuine truths in my life. One was the Diamond Mountains (Keum Kang San) and the other was Dosan. To begin with, he was very handsome. He didn't look like a great hero,

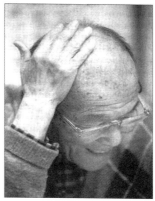

Pi Chun-deuk

but a simple man with a warm, kind face. His voice was very vibrant but clear and tender with no sharp edge to it... a magnetic and attractive voice. I have heard President Franklin D. Roosevelt speak, who was supposed to have a marvelous voice, but he was no match for Dosan. He was one in a million, his appearance, his voice, and his heart were unequaled in quality. He stunned an audience with a speech on government corruption given in Pyongyang near the Dae Dong River when he was twenty or so years old. He became a remarkable leader from that point on. I always thought that he was a great man, and he never disappointed me. He was truthful and earnest, and treated everyone with respect. He had many followers and he made each one of us feel very special."

There is a reason why "love" has become a foundation for leadership in recent years. First, "love" is the basis for human relations. To become a leader, one must accurately assess his or her strengths and weaknesses, and further develop his strengths and make every effort to correct his weaknesses. One must "like" himself in order to do this and sustain his sense of self-worth. A leader should not fall into the trap of hating himself and lose sight of the direction for him and the group.

As it was mentioned earlier, Dosan believed that love was the basic ingredient in building harmonious relationships and, that it flowed naturally when one respected others and supported them. Love is often said to have a "high rate of transmission" in that it is easily recognized by those who are on the receiving end, including animals and plants. Dogs, man's closest friend in the animal world, react favorably to love and affection. Plants do better when they are loved and cared for. It goes without saying that humans, the most advanced beings on earth, should recognize and react to love more readily than animals and plants.

Love serves as an impetus for generating power and strength in operating an organization. Love and respect among members of an organization generate tremendous strength and power, as it has been proven at times of crisis for nations and organizations. Dosan preached and acted on this principle.

Dosan believed that "love of self" must precede "love of others" and one must reform himself before he could reform others. "Love of self" is rooted in the principle that "I" is the center of the universe and that we come to realize how it feels to be at the center of the universe. Then we learn that others feel the same way we do. Further, we learn what others expect from us, that is, they want to be treated just the same way we would want to be treated. So we first give them what they want, listen to them before we expect them to listen to us, and support them before we expect them to give us support.

Dosan's "sense of proprietorship" is also based on the philosophy that "all things begin with me." I am the center of the universe; therefore I behave proactively and care for it as if the world belongs to me. This self-centered thinking may be misconstrued as selfishness at the outset. However, what Dosan actually had in mind was for his students and colleagues to develop a sense of love for others through love of self, thereby acquiring leadership skills, namely "leading by serving" his constituents. Dosan wanted nothing in return for his love for his fellow countrymen. Love of his country was the way he lived his life in words and in action until the day he died.

Leadership by Love: Love Makes Everything Grow.

- Love became central to Dosan's value system because of his
  - inherent character
  - Christian education at Miller Academy
  - his experience in American society

- Self improvement is predicated on love of self.

- Love is a prerequisite for respecting the other's opinion and caring.

- When members of an organization love each other, the organization generates its power.

2
Sharing Love

Geese fly in a "V" formation traveling thousands of miles southward every fall in preparation for winter. And they return North in the spring. Tom Worsham, author of *Are You a Goose* writes, "When you see geese heading south for the winter flying along in a "V" formation, you might be interested in knowing that science has discovered why they fly that way. Research has revealed that as each bird flaps its wings, it creates uplift for the bird immediately behind it. By flying in a "V" formation, the whole flock adds at least 71 percent greater flying range than if each bird flew on its own.

Whenever a goose falls out of formation, it

A flock of geese traveling long distance

suddenly feels the drag and resistance of trying to go it alone. It quickly gets back into formation to take advantage of the lifting power of the bird immediately in front. When the lead goose gets tired, he rotates back in the "V" and another goose flies the point.

The geese honk from behind to encourage those up front to keep up their speed. And finally, when a goose gets sick, or is wounded by gunfire and falls out, two other geese falls out of formation and follow it down to help and protect it. They stay with the goose until it is either able to fly again or dead, and then they launch out on their own or with another formation to catch up with their group."

Dosan saw early on the lessons for group life that geese held and adopted the goose as the symbol for the Hungsadan. He wrote that the leader did not need to be smarter or stronger than everyone, but needed to be someone who was willing to go to the head of the group. Once the leader is chosen, the members should support and encourage the leader rather than tearing him down. The leader is not one who exercises his power over the group, but someone who works more than anyone else on behalf of the group. In other words, the leading goose is not there to exercise his power over the group, but to serve the group. So, when the leading goose determines that he is unable to lead the group, he does not hesitate to drift backward and take a position in the formation. This is the type of democratic leadership Dosan envisioned. Again, "love" is the impetus for the leaders' willingness to block the wind for his fellow geese and the rest of the flock encourage and support their leader out of love.

A male goose and a female goose mate for life. Presenting a goose to newlyweds has long been a Korean custom. The goose represents a long and happy life together for the couple. Nowadays a pair of wooden geese is sometimes given to the newlyweds as a symbol for a married life of one hundred years. A guideline written for women (Gyu Hap Chong Seo) during the latter part of the Joseon Dynasty records the symbolic value of the geese as following:

"Geese have four virtues. First, they stand for 'reliability,' because they fly south when it is cold and fly north when it is warm in amazing regularity. Two, they stand for courtesy because they communicate with each other, from the front to the rear and the rear to the front. Third, they stand for fidelity because they do not seek a new mate when the old one dies. Fourth, they stand for wisdom because they take turns and stand watch while they sleep at night, and during the day, they hang on to reeds to avoid hunters. These are the reasons why the bride presents the groom's parents with a goose."

Sharing Love: Leadership Lessons from Geese

① Teamwork produces better results.
② A leader is someone who serves the rest of the group.
③ Members continually send encouragement to the leader.
④ When the leader tires, the next one takes over the leadership position.
⑤ They help those who fall behind.
⑥ Love is central to life.

3
East Meets West

Confucianism has left a profound influence on Korean life ever since it was introduced to Korea almost two thousand years ago. Confucianism, together with Buddhism, became the ideological and spiritual foundation for Koreans. It was in the 17th century that the Eastern culture met the predominantly Christian West. Cardinal Kim Su-hwan describes the difference between the two: "Koreans subscribed to Confucian thoughts then, whereby people focused on '*Hyo*' (devotion) for their parents and projected it up to the supreme being of the heavens, while the Christian teachings directed the devotion to the Lord first then down to the parents."

Dosan was a Christian but embraced other religions as well. He learned traditional studies highlighting Confucian ways until he was sixteen years old, when he entered Miller Hak Dahng (Academy), a Christian missionary school in Seoul. Hence he became a Christian and adopted its philosophy of "love thy neighbor." He deplored his fellow Koreans for favoring Confucian sophistry rather than engaging in productive actions, and urged them to practice more love and respect in their daily lives. He favored many Christian ways, yet he allowed his Hungsadan members to follow their own faith instead of insisting on Christianity.

Dosan's Ae Ki Ae Ta philosophy is the result of the Christian "love" concept, the Confucian "*hyo*" concept and moral virtue, and the Buddhist concept of "equal charity and good will for all people." Christ preached love for all people, strangers and enemies alike, but Dosan's love began with family members, i.e., love between husband and wife, and father and son. Dosan's Ae Ki Ae Ta focuses on love, while Confucianism is more about social order and established customs. Dosan sought to change what he deemed "a society without love and affection" into an "affectionate" one by way of extending the familial love to the society and to the nation.

Dosan understood early that the time had come for East and West to combine and create a new value system for humankind. Dosan's concept of "Jong Ui" (meaning warm friendship) is easier for plain folks to fathom and execute than the Christian "love" that demands unconditional devotion and sacrifice beyond their reach.

Dosan picking oranges at an orchard in Riverside, California

In other words, Dosan made it simpler for an average person to practice good will without becoming a devoted Christian. One simply needed to remember to respect others; earn and maintain their trust; and be courteous to others. Dosan believed that people could train themselves to become a better person in realistic terms. In this sense he was a realist rather than a religious person. Training is easier said than done, however, and Dosan looked to Buddhist training methods. He practiced meditation, as witnessed by Susan Ahn, his oldest daughter. As a youngster, she would peek through the door to his study and watch him meditate for hours. "He would sit in his room in his yoga position for hours without moving a hair. I had no idea what he was doing but we didn't dare disturb him."

He was practicing meditation, training his heart and mind toward enlightenment. Most likely, four *brahma-viharas* — *metta* (friendliness or loving-kindness), compassion, sympathetic joy, and even-mindedness — were the subject of his meditation to increase these qualities in himself and those around him.

French novelist Antoine de Saint Exupéry writing about another world addresses similar concerns in his book *The Little Prince*. The fox teaches the prince how to deal with people, how to become familiar with them, and how to love them. The fox shares his secret of life: "One sees clearly only with the heart. The essential is invisible to the eyes."

Dosan emphasizes three elements in his article entitled "Today's Students of Korea" in *Dong Gwang* magazine in 1926: one, nurturing patriotic spirit and sacrificing oneself whether anyone knows about it or not; two, nurturing sympathy for those who are less fortunate than us; three, learning and practicing cooperative spirit. Dosan took the best of all three religions and molded them into a practical solution unique to Korean society.

Cardinal Kim Su-hwan once observed that, in Korea, Confucianism, Buddhism, and Christianity coexist in harmony and this unique condition could offer humanity a new, spiritual light.

Leo Buscaglia, the first person to lecture about love as a formal study said that cultures and religions around the world are different from each other, but love is the common element in human relations. Love is the common language for all people. Further, love should be unconditional, just as Dosan preached the value of serving one's organization without considering his own individual gain. One hundred years later Kent Keith, the renowned leadership expert, also points out the importance of "serving without condition."

Leadership has long been a subject of study. It is based on research materials and books written by Dale Carnegie, Steven Covey, and Warren Bennis, among others. It is time to formalize Dosan's teachings into the field of leadership studies because of what he has to offer in terms of spiritual gain for humanity, as Cardinal Kim Su-hwan points out. In formulating Ae Ki Ae Ta, Dosan combined the best elements from three religions and created a new spiritual guide.

Dale Carnegie addressed the technical skills in acquiring influence over people, while Dosan was concerned about the fundamental philosophy of leadership. In addition, Dosan applied his philosophy to everyday life in specific terms, showing Hungsadan members how to become leaders for the work of the independence movement.

East Meets West

- Dosan's Ae Ki Ae Ta philosophy is the result of the Christian "love" concept, the Confucian "hyo" concept and moral virtue, and the Buddhist concept of "equal charity and good will for all people."

- Dosan adapted the western concept of "noblesse oblige" for forming his basic ideology for Hungsadan group.

- The Ae Ki Ae Ta leadership is unique in that Dosan combined the eastern thought process and western methodology.

- This combination of the East and the West provides an expanded platform for addressing human conditions worldwide.

4
Gift of Ae Ki Ae Ta Leadership

So far we have covered various types of leadership and how the effectiveness of respective methods would vary according to the situations. We also pointed out that, in a democratic society, service leadership is more effective than the power leadership.

Ae Ki Ae Ta leadership can be regarded as either a service or servant leadership as defined by Kent Keith due to its "ethical, practical, and meaningful" content. Servant leaders feel tremendous satisfaction from the ethical and meaningful aspects of leadership, and organizations can reap more benefits from this. Consequently, results oriented business leaders as well as military leaders are now keen on servant leadership. In the following section, we would like to introduce what results Ae Ki Ae Ta could bring.

4.1 Increase the Level of Self-Satisfaction Through Meaningfulness

Man constantly searches for the meaning of life, asking questions like "Who am I? Why do I exist?" These have been crucial questions for philosophers and thinkers for centuries, and for anyone who enters adult age or becomes old enough to ponder about his or her future. So, we humans become motivated when we think that our work is meaningful and worthwhile. Viktor Frankl, the author of *Man's Search for Meaning*, also a psychologist who spent time in a Nazi concentration camp, writes about survivors. He saw that people with the desire to make future plans had a better chance for survival. Based on his experience from the concentration camp, he devised a therapy called logotherapy to help people search and find meanings in their lives. Meanings that people seek in their lives are different for everyone, but what is important is the act of search itself.

Research shows that people who believe that they are leading meaningful lives are healthier mentally as well as physicalhy. Professor Edward Deci, an expert on self-motivation, conducted a study of a graduating class at Rochester University in New York and discovered that students interested in meaningful relationships, volunteering, and self-improvement were more vibrant and happy than those students who were interested in wealth, appearance, and recognition. Introspective people tend to look inward and depend on their own views and attitudes for their lives.

Richard Layard, author of *Happiness: The Lessons from a New Science*, supports the theory that people with positive attitudes about human relationships, self-improvement, and the meaning of life feel happier than those who look for temporary pleasure. People who find their meaning of life are happier because they are doing what they want to do.

Tal Ben-Shahar, professor of psychology at Harvard University and author of *Happier* says,

"Happiness lies at the intersection between pleasure and meaning. Happiness results when we are engaged in both pleasurable activities and those which are aligned with purpose... we need more than just instant gratification. We need a sense of purpose. A human being, like a business, makes profits and suffers losses. For a human being, however, the ultimate currency is not money, nor is it any external measure, such as fame, fortune or power. The ultimate currency for a human being is happiness."

Then, where do people find their meaning in life? Kent Keith conducted a survey of 3,500 people and found that they based their meaning of life in families, exchange of love, close relationships, doing their best, and sense of accomplishment. In terms of scale of importance, things like wealth, power, fame, and victory scored well below what was expected. The survey showed that, for most people, the most important items were to love and help others.

Dosan Ahn Chang-Ho suggests that we use maternal love as a model for our attitude toward others and that we apply the same attitude to managing the organizations to which we belong. Buddhist monk

Beop Jeong (1932–2010), also the author of a spiritual book *MuSoYu* (No Possession), talks about maternal love:

> "There's nothing purer than the warmth of a mother's love for her child. A mother and child are forever connected by an unbreakable bond beginning with the umbilical cord. So we talk about our mother in our final moment on earth, and the world's cruelest criminal sheds tears in front of his mother. We become pure beings in front of our mother because our mother is the origin of life."

4.2 Recycling Good Will: Impetus for Cooperation and Change

Beop Jeong said, "Truth echoes." The same is true for love. When we give love to someone, it always comes back as an echo of love. This is the principle of recycling the goodwill of love. In other words, love begets love, blessing begets blessing, sympathy begets sympathy, sharing begets sharing, and happiness begets happiness. This is recycling the goodwill of love. Therefore, we must find the language of love and spread it throughout the world.

Buddhist monk Beop Jeong

So we must grow our ability to love. Erich Fromm (1900–1980), the author of *The Art of Loving*, presents love as a skill that can be taught and developed. Fromm observes that real love "is not a sentiment which can be easily indulged in by anyone." It is only through developing one's total personality to the capacity of loving one's neighbor with "true humility, courage, faith and discipline" that one acquires the capacity to experience real love.

Fromm's idea of love mirrors that of Dosan. Dosan encouraged his disciples to "endlessly train to love."

Then, what is the language of love? There is a variety of means to practice love. Dosan's favorite English word was "smile." Smiling is a strong language of love. There is a Korean adage, "You can't spit at someone who is smiling," meaning that a smile is very infectious. We experience the effectiveness of smiling in our daily lives. When we smile at a stranger in elevators or in passing on streets, they respond with a smile as well, dissolving any awkwardness that may exist. Saint Exupéry writes about exchanging smiles with his prison guard when he was captured during the war. The smile led to genuine conversations with the guard, which then led to his escape from certain death.

A smile graduates into laughter. It is said that laughter is an expression of satisfaction. Early on, psychologist Sigmund Freud defined laughter as a means to release tension and psychic energy. Norman Cousins, a journalist, speaks about his miraculous recovery from his untreatable disease by watching comedy films and reading humorous books. He wrote a book entitled *Anatomy of an Illness as Perceived by the Patient.* He concludes that laughter dissipates fear and anger that are poison to the patient, not to mention boredom.

A baby is said to start laughing about seventeen days after birth, well before he learns to speak. A child laughs over three hundred times a day, while an adult may laugh fifteen times on an average day. A patient in a hospital does not laugh at all. In short, it can be said that we humans lose the ability to laugh as we become adults. It is important to recover our ability to smile and laugh... our language of love.

Next, let's talk about "listening," another effective language of love. American poet Oliver Wendell Holmes (1809–1894) said, "It is the province of knowledge to speak, and it is the privilege of wisdom to listen," meaning that listening is an effective tool for forming an agreement, more so than trying to explain one's position until he is blue in the face. This is the reason why corporations and political organizations turn to listening as a successful methodology. For example, the Chairman of Samsung Corporation, Lee Gun-hee, adopted listening as the corporate theme, inspired by his father's calligraphy. People who have the opportunity to visit Lee at his home enthusiastically talk about his penchant to listen rather than to speak about himself. People are said to be impressed by his ability to listen.

Praising is another wonderful language of love. Dale Carnegie said that praise even melts iron, and "Any fool can criticize, condemn, and complain — and most fools do."

The inscription on Andrew Carnegie's tombstone says, "Here lays a man who knew how to enlist the service of better men than him." In other words, Andrew Carnegie knew how to praise, his language of love. Ken Blanchard, wrote a book entitled, *Whale Done!* describing the method used to train whales to perform incredible acts. Attention and encouragement do wonders for whales, and we can imagine what attention and encouragement do for our fellow human beings. Happy people lead happy organizations, and praise makes everyone happy.

Furthermore, smiling, listening, and praising must be done in earnest. That is very important. People can readily pick up on insincere smiles, unsympathetic ears, and empty praise. In other words, the language of love, to be effective, must contain love. In the end, love is the crucial element, and, if there is love, one can generate the language of love depending on situations. The language of love can be an impetus for recycling the goodwill of love and can bring cooperation and change.

Gifts that Ae Ki Ae Ta Leadership Brings to the World

① It increases the level of self-satisfaction.
② It creates motivation when performing meaningful tasks.
③ By giving love, one receives love in return, as in an echo.
④ It creates an impetus for recycling love and effects cooperation and change.

5

Seven Tasks for Ae Ki Ae Ta Leader

In Chapter Two, we discussed ten items related to the formation of Ae Ki Ae Ta leadership in terms of management of self, human relations, and management of organization. In Chapter Three, we emphasized the fact that Ae Ki Ae Ta leadership begins with love. We discovered that Dosan's Ae Ki Ae Ta spirit is founded on Christian love, together with Buddhist compassion and Confucian "hyo." It is an amalgamation of values from the East and the West.

Here, let us take a look at what an Ae Ki Ae Ta leader must do, now that we know the principle behind it. When we ask the question, "What should Ae Ki Ae Ta leaders do?" we can find the answer by studying what Dosan did. When Dosan was twenty-four-years old, he came to America to study, only to find the pitiful living conditions of his fellow Koreans residing in San Francisco. He persuaded them to change their ways of thinking and living. He helped Koreans in America improve their lives and then went on to China to help establish the Provisional Government of Korea. He displayed tremendous leadership ability, at a time when other leaders, such as Philip Jaisohn and Syngman Rhee were both much more educated and experienced. Dosan was the one who actually improved the lives of fellow Koreans, guiding them with his Ae Ki Ae Ta spirit and acting on its principles.

5.1 Sharing Trust by Honesty and Sincerity

Honesty is the first quality that Ae Ki Ae Ta leaders must attain. The first reason Dosan accomplished this monumental task was that he earned the trust of his fellow Koreans through his honesty and sincerity. According to people who met Dosan, the strongest impression they have of him was his honesty and righteousness. Philip Jaisohn, who was older than Dosan, regarded Dosan as a person of high morals with a big heart, and he considered Dosan as his role model. Also, Yi Kwang-su, one of Dosan's disciples, wrote that Dosan was straight as an arrow without fault. Essayist Pi Chun-deuk, who compared Dosan to the Diamond Mountains, wrote about Dosan's morals:

> "His life was simply the truth. He probably never has lied in his life. We always run across situations in which we have to lie for good cause. I recall him saying, 'You can lie only when truth would cause great harm for your comrade. But it's better to keep silent and say nothing.' That's what he told me."

Thus Dosan's honesty left an everlasting impression on people.

5.2 Accumulating Knowledge; Trustworthy Knowledge Is More Powerful

Dosan's philosophy is often referred to as a "philosophy of power." This is because Dosan repeatedly talked about the "lack of power" that caused Korea to lose its sovereignty to imperial Japan, and he exhorted people to develop individual power in order to recover the nation. He was referring to empowerment of the people. Dosan taught his disciples that all things on earth, tangible or intangible, are products of a power consisting of certain forces and energy. He believed that great power could accomplish great things, and that weak power would accomplish small things.

As we mentioned it earlier, he believed that a "wholesome character" and "solid unity" were prerequisites to generating personal power, and further, he emphasized the importance for each person to learn and develop one or more fields of expertise. If that was too hard to achieve, he said, then one should have at least one practical skill, and he pointed out that his skill was in house-cleaning. He encouraged the young people to seek practical knowledge and skills instead of the popular traditional esoteric study based on Confucianism. He was one of the early proponents of modern education and knowledge. He also pushed everyone, individual or organization, to become economically sound, realizing that economic well-being was the foundation for his "power" concept. Dosan built organizations and at the same time he promoted industrial projects.

When Dosan founded Jom Jin School, he simultaneously embarked on a land development project. He spoke about modernizing homes and building model farms to his colleagues at the Tae Geuk Hak Hoe (research institute) in Tokyo in 1907 on his way to Korea. When he built the Dae Sung School, he founded the first public joint stockholding corporation in Korea, a ceramics manufacturing and distribution company. He established a company called Tae Geuk Publishing Company and the Tae Geuk bookstore chain. He also initiated Asia Industries, Inc., which later developed into Tae Dong Industries, Inc. with a substantial capitalization of $50,000. In 1910, when he was thirty-two years old, he put together an economic association with Koreans in Siberia. In 1912, he founded North American Industries, Inc. in California with a capitalization of $45,000.

As the Prime Minister for the Provincial Government of Korea in 1919, he issued government bonds and focused on raising funds for the independence movement. In his later years, he worked on building a base for independence work and organizing model communities in Manchuria, until 1931 when Japan invaded Manchuria.

In all of these economic activities, Dosan worked hard to build trust among all parties. There would not be any economic transactions or growth without mutual trust. If honesty is the foundation for trust among individuals, then mutual trust forms the foundation for companies to work together. He espoused the importance of building "communal trust" together.

Dosan thought that military power was effective in the short term, but not in the long term. Economic power was a must for building the military as well as for attaining the independence of Korea. Consequently, he steadily worked on developing human resources and economic opportunities, emphasizing the importance of knowledge and trust. This is the second lesson for Ae Ki Ae Ta leaders.

5.3 Identifying Visions and Goals

The third element for Ae Ki Ae Ta leaders to remember is to develop the ability to see ahead and properly set visions and goals for themselves and for the organization.

We mentioned earlier that Dosan had three dreams: Korean independence, an economically strong Korea, and respect for Koreans from people around the world. These were ambitious dreams, to say the least, considering that the Koreans were under the colonial rule of Japan.

As remote as the possibilities were, Dosan was able to form his vision because he could read what was going on in the world. He knew that strong nations around the world were engaged in expansionism, competing against each other with their economic wealth and military forces. He urged that "we must understand how the power game works in order to survive the age of imperialism." All the while he never lost his belief that "Justice ultimately prevails" and that despite Japan's attempt at cultural cleansing in Korea, such as prohibiting the use of the Korean language, Japan would not be able to keep Korea under oppression.

Nevertheless, he set a high vision and goals for Korea because he saw the big picture. His contemporaries thought that military resistance was the only effective way to battle Japanese imperialism, and he supported that view. However, he stressed that "We must not stop at the military effort. We must go a step further and develop the ability to run our nation when we achieve independence."

Ito Hirobumi (1841–1909), the first Japanese Resident General of Korea, suggested to Dosan in 1907, "Let us form a cabinet together and do great things for Korea. Then we can proceed on to China together, and eventually build a Great Asia on our own instead of giving it to the Westerners." Dosan saw through Ito's offer and realized that Ito was only interested in using him and replied, "I am only interested in an independent Korea as a sovereign nation. You should help us become an independent nation just as you helped your own country." Dosan denied Ito's request right away because he could see the bigger picture and caught on to Japan's imperialistic ambitions to conquer Asia. Dosan was correct in reading Japan's intention to dominate Asia. As feared, Japan forcibly annexed Korea in 1910 and then went on to invade China, the Philippines, Singapore, and Burma.

In the meantime, Koreans split into two ideological camps, one being the socialist left, and the other the nationalist right, who were supporters of a democratic form of government. The political factions went at each other instead of teaming up together for independence work. Dosan worked very hard to get them to unify, but they couldn't see beyond their own ideological blinders. Sadly, the same divisive argument is still going on today between North Korea and South Korea, exactly contrary to what Dosan had wished for. If anyone could bring the two sides together, it would be Dosan. Had he lived ten years longer, the Korean peninsula would not be divided in two.

How was it that Dosan could see things so far

ahead of time? He was a rational man with tremendous insight into human nature. He respected intellectual theories, but he also respected the wisdom and common sense of real people on the street. In his search for solutions to problems, he always looked deep into human nature for answers rather than what appeared just on the surface.

5.4 Making Detailed Plans

Meticulous planning then is the fourth item for the Ae Ki Ae Ta leader. Dosan followed up with detailed plans for his visions and goals. Organizing the Hungsadan was the prime example of his planning of the direction and strategy for solving Korea's independence problem.

In the memos that Dosan wrote in 1913, we can see that he planned for an organization to lead the independence movement and recruited potential leaders. He taught them patience, courage, loyalty, and fellowship, using these principles for uniting its members. The members of the organization became a unit that behaved with consistency, and they had a clear understanding of their roles, and a unified ideology.

In defining the tasks for the independence movement, Dosan divided the overall independence work into two main stages, the preparatory stage and the completion stage. The preparatory stage was carried out by the scholastic group and the executive group. The completion stage consisted of the independence militia, a cabinet, politicians, engineers, doctors, businessmen, and teachers who would carry out tasks necessary for the independence work. He earmarked the treasury funds for military equipment, military organization, military provisions, construction expenses, and diplomacy expenses. The completion stage was divided into two sub-stages: first, the initiation of an independence war against Japan and the formation of the political and military command to lead the war effort; and second, the reconstruction of the nation following the war.

Dosan's ability to strategize is well demonstrated in the organization and operation of the Hungsadan, especially in the second clause of the Hungsadan charter, which states: "The purpose of the Hungsadan is to unite loyal men and women willing to devote their lives to Mu Shil Yeok Hang (pursuit of truths; vigorously acting on them) in the name of justice. Further, the members will train together in three areas of discipline — virtue, physical strength, and knowledge — and build wholesome characters, and form a sacred unity, thereby preparing a foundation for the greatest undertaking of our people."

In these words we can read the elements of the Ae Ki Ae Ta spirit and see Dosan's priority in building a team of high caliber people to lead the independence movement. To that end, he meticulously prepared the procedure for recruiting members, especially the long, rigorous question and answer membership interview process that was designed for potential candidates to focus on the purpose of their lives as well as their vision for the nation.

Dosan's strategy for the independence movement (1913)

Completion

National Advancement   Recovery of sovereignty

In progress

Form new political system   Independence war

Complete preparation

Manpower   Finance

Independence army   Army base
Ministers   Army supplies
Politicians   Army provisions
Engineers   Construction cost
Doctors   Diplomacy cost
Businessmen
Academicians

Preparation in progress

Academics   Business

Cooperative schools   Individual enterprise
(Information & books)   Financial entities exchange
Ethical training   Cooperatives
Intellectual training   Manufacturing
Athletic training   Commercial trading
Vocational schools   Agriculture
All disciplines

Foundation

Unity   Mental power

Trust   United ideology
Loyalty   Division of labor
Courage   Consistent action
Patience

5.5 Passionate Execution

"Walking the walk" is the fifth item on list of tasks for Ae Ki Ae Ta leaders. Dosan was a man of action, someone we would now refer to as "a man who walked the walk." In organizing the political system for the independence movement, he also backed it up with economic plans, as well as founding schools and organizations at the same time. At the age of twenty, he established a western branch office of the Mahn Min (ten thousand people) Gong Dong Hoi (Community Association) along with the Jom Jin (Deliberate Progress) School and the Dahn Po Ri Church, as well as land development projects. When he was about thirty years-old he organized a secret, hardcore vigilante group called the Shin Min Hoi (the New People's Association), along with Dae Sung (Great success) School, as well as the Masan Ceramics Company. At thirty-five years of age, he organized the Korean National Association (KNA) in the United States, along with the North American Industries Corporation for generating economic resources, as well as the Hungsadan and the Claremont Student Center in order to develop manpower. At age forty, when he was appointed the Prime Minister of the Korean Provisional Government, he sought to establish business interests, and he served as a principal of the In Sung School in Shanghai. Wherever he went, he was very active in creating various tools for the independence movement, namely, political, economic, and educational entities. This required real passion for his fatherland, as well as the ability to inspire others to have the same passion. Dosan clearly had both passions. While under arrest in a Japanese prison, he told his interrogators, "My work is the independence movement, and I only think about the independence of Korea, even in my sleep and when I eat my meals." His passion for his fatherland was legendary, and this passion carried him through all his difficult times, multiple incarcerations and relentless torture. This passion allowed him to consistently move forward in his endeavors.

5.6 Practicing Love and Making It a Habit

Love is the main theme for Ae Ki Ae Ta. Accordingly, Ae Ki Ae Ta leaders must treat the members of their organization with love. Yi Kwang-su, Dosan's close disciple and biographer wrote about Dosan's use of the word "love" under the topic, "Love for comrades and a world filled with love for each other." Yi wrote:

> "He would recite the words — 'Let us study love, you and I. Men, women of twenty million… let us all study about love. And become a nation of people who love each other' — as though he were reciting a poem or singing a song with unbridled emotion."

Yi writes that "Dosan was having a love affair with the Korean people. When he was boasting about the strong points of Koreans he was very happy, and when he talked about their weaknesses, he looked so sad and pained like he was being tortured." We can see in this statement Dosan's passion for his fellow countrymen. In the question and answer process for the Hungsadan recruits he spent the majority of time evaluating their love for their fellow countrymen and for their country. He wanted to make sure that they understood the importance of love. He strongly believed that justice and love were more important for the survival of an organization, rather than the organization's ideology. Dosan repeatedly said, "We will live if we love each other, and die if we fight against each other. Let's treat all of our Dong Po (fellow countrymen) with love, even those whom we consider evil."

Toward the end of his life, he built a retreat called Song Tae Sahn Jahng (Great Pine Mountain Villa) where he spent his final years until his last detention in a Japanese prison in Seoul. He'd received his visitors at Song Tae and told them, "We should build a world where everyone smiles (bing gu ray) with affection for each other." This is where Dosan himself wrote the words Ae Ki Ae Ta in a calligraphy which he sent to his family in America.

Yi Kwang-su concludes Dosan's biography with "Dosan wanted to build a nation of smiles. He trained himself to love and smile, and urged his comrades to do the same. 'Warm heart, smiling faces' was the picture

Dosan envisioned for his countrymen, and he dearly wished that his countrymen would achieve this whether it took a hundred years or a thousand years." Likewise, love became the main theme in Yi Kwang-su's literary works as well.

Love truly is the foundation for his Ae Ki Ae Ta leadership, and we should follow his example and sincerely train to make love our habit.

5.7 Serving with a Sense of Ownership and Love

The next element Dosan considered important was the sense of ownership. He wrote an article entitled, "A Presentation to My Fellow Koreans" in the *Dong-A Ilbo* in January 1925, and another, entitled, "Are You an Owner?" in the June issue of *Dong Gwang* magazine in 1926. In both of these articles, he questioned the readers, "How many people among us consider themselves as owners of our society?" and enumerated that an owner is one who feels responsible for the community and for the society. If not, he asserted, the person is no more than a mere visitor.

Dosan stated further, "No matter how capable we feel, how rich or knowledgeable we feel, we must do our best in our planning and maintaining our home till the day we die… and that is how a real owner behaves."

In Chapter Two earlier, we talked about Greenleaf's concept of servant leadership. We also discussed Herman Hesse's book, *Journey to the East* and its main character by the name of Leo. Leo, disguised as the servant for the travel group, was the real owner and master of the League which sponsored the journey. As a servant, he cared for the group and handled all the details of the journey. The journey went smoothly and pleasantly for everyone until Leo disappeared from the scene. Without Leo, the trip turned into chaos, and they had to abandon the journey in the middle of it. Leo proved the value of servant leadership. Dosan made the same point with his Ae Ki Ae Ta leadership. Ae Ki Ae Ta leaders should practice becoming servant leaders, thereby serving their organization with love and the pride of ownership.

Seven Tasks for Ae Ki Ae Ta Leader

① Build trust within the organization by exercising honesty and sincerity.
② Strengthen the organization by the power of knowledge and trust.
③ Identify visions and goals.
④ Formulate detailed plans.
⑤ Execute plans with passion.
⑥ Practice love and make it a habit.
⑦ Serve the organization with a sense of ownership and love.

The Future of the Ae Ki Ae Ta Leadership

For two centuries following the industrial revolution which began in the 18th and 19th century, the world saw the "Era of the Atlantic Ocean," meaning that Western Europe and the East Coast region of the United States were the hubs of the activities in commerce, trade, and politics. Come the 21st century, the world is now seeing the shift to the "Era of the Pacific Ocean," a new hub spreading across the West Coast of the American continent and North East Asia, namely, China, Korea, and Japan.

In view of the latest monetary crisis across the globe and China's ascent up the world's economic ladder, we see a real shift of power to the Pacific. Korea is in the middle of that power as it has hosted the G20 event and facilitated the formation of a new monetary order for the world. A close ally of the United States, Korea is one of the main players in the

Pacific region, and is geographically positioned in between the other major players, China and Japan, who are friendly nations to Korea as well.

The main engine for the 21st century is the IT (Information Technology) industry. In the United States, Silicon Valley has emerged as the center of the IT industry, thereby shifting the focus to the West Coast. Korea also has emerged as one of the leaders in the IT industry. But for Korea to assume a lead role in the Pacific Era, technological skills and economic prowess alone are not sufficient. Korea needs to produce leaders who can bridge the East and the West, accommodating the needs of the developed nations and developing nations. The ability to act as a hub for the 21st century is not possible using power-centered leadership, but through implementing the servant leadership model based on the sense of ownership and love.

The 21st century is also referred to as the era of fusion or convergence. In the technology sector, IT (Information Technology) is fusing with BT (Bio Tech) and mechanical engineering and creating new technologies. In the social science sector, executives are fusing the management field with the design field, the hospital field, and the welfare field, and pioneering new fields such as design management, hospital management, and welfare management.

In the field of leadership, we are seeing more and more fusion of Eastern and Western philosophies, as well as the fusion of the business administration field and the psychology field. The Ae Ki Ae Ta principle represents the fusion of most of the elements contained in modern leadership studies and best explains the latest concept of servant leadership

The Gyeonggi Welfare Foundation invited Kent Keith, director of Greenleaf Servant Leadership Center, to visit Korea in December 2009 and held a seminar to compare and analyze the Servant Leadership concept and Dosan's Ae Ki Ae Ta leadership. The seminar concluded with an agreement that both concepts share the same fundamental spirit, despite the difference in time, place of origins and the means of dissemination. Author Suh Sang-mok presented a paper on Ae Ki Ae Ta leadership at the International Servant Leadership Conference in Atlanta in June 2010, in an effort to introduce the concept in the international arena. At present, the Dosan Memorial Foundation is conducting a class in Seoul to teach the youth about Ae Ki Ae Ta leadership, and plans to extend the educational opportunity overseas. We strongly feel that we have a mission to carry on the work of Dosan Ahn Chang-Ho and to pass on his Ae Ki Ae Ta leadership model to future generations to help accomplish his vision and to turn his dream into a reality.

Chronology of Dosan's Leadership

Dosan and his family, 1917

1878

November 9 Born on Dorong Island, 7-li Chori ward, GangSeo county of PyongNam Province (now North Korea) as the third son of father Ahn Heung Kuk (Kyo Jin) (of the Sunhung Ahn clan) and mother Hwang Mongun (of the Osong Hwang clan) of JeAhn. (His oldest brother was Ahn Chi Ho, his second older brother died young (maybe Ahn Chi Yong), and his sister was Ahn Shin Ho (born in 1884).

1885

Seven years old, he begins his schooling in traditional Chinese studies at Guk Su Dang on the shores of Dae Dong River in Pyongyang. He works as a shepherd.

Dae Dong River, circa 1880

1889

Ahn Heung Kuk, Dosan's father, died when Dosan was eleven years old.

1891

Thirteen years old, he learns Chinese from Master Kim Hyun Jin at a village school where he meets Pil Dae Eun (from Anak,

Hwanghea Province), who introduces him to new ways of looking at the world.

1894

Sixteen years old, he goes to Seoul and enters the Miller Academy (on Sobudae Jong-dong in Seoul) and studies English, Western Civilization, and Christianity. He converts to the Presbyterian Church, and he convinces Pil Dae Eun to become a Christian as well. (Miller Academy was originally called the Underwood Academy.)

Principal Miller

When Dosan attended the school, Rev. F.S. Miller was the principal, thus the name change to Miller Academy. After Dosan graduated, the school was called Gu Se (Salvation) Academy, and later changed to Kyung Shin (New Respect) School.

1896

Eighteen years old, he continues to study at the Miller Academy and works as a teaching assistant. (This year the Independence) Newspaper (Tong Nip Shin Mun)

Miller Academy students and teachers

Independence Club magazine and *The Independence* Newspaper

was first published by Philip Jaisohn (aka Soh Jae Pil); and, the
Independence Association (Tong Nip Hyup Hoe) was formed.)

1897

Nineteen years old, he joins Philip
Jaisohn's Independence Association
and establishes its West Pyongyang
branch of Mahn Min Gong
Dong Hoe (Ten Thousand People
Community Association)

Dosan (middle) as a member of
Independence Club

1898

Twenty years old, he made the Quae Jae Jung speech for the
Pan National Coalition. His speech consisted of "18 satisfactory
pieces of news and 18 unsatisfactory pieces of news." This
speech distinguishes him as a superb orator. Later that year, he
makes a speech in JongNo, Seoul, criticizing seven officials in
the King's court who signed the Korea-Japan New Agreement,

and, suggests six items for political reform. He is engaged to marry Lee Hye Ryon (later Helen Ahn) daughter of his former teacher Lee Sukbo. His fiancée and sister go to Seoul to attend Jongshin Girl's School.

December 1898, the Independence Association was shut down by King Gojong.

1899

Twenty-one years old, he establishes Jeom Jin (Deliberate Progress) School in Amhwa Village Dongjin ward, Gang Seo County Pyongnam Province. Jeom Jin was the first modern school in the county, and the first coeducational school in Korea. Ahn Chang Ho initiates a land development company and establishes Dan Po Ri Church (Later Ki Yang Church).

1902

Twenty-four years old, he marries Lee Hye Ryon at Je Jung Won (House of Universal Helpfulness) Hospital in Seoul, arranged by Kim Yoono (Maria Kim's uncle) and conducted by Reverend Miller. (September 3.) He and

Je Jung Won Hospital where Dosan and Helen Ahn were married

his wife embark for America to study education. (September 4.) They spend one week in Tokyo. Near the Hawaiian Islands, he coins his penname Dosan. They arrive in San Francisco, California. (October 14) He enrolls in a public elementary school and works as a houseboy in San Francisco.

1903

Twenty-five years old, he organizes Han In Chin Mok Hoe (Korean Friendship Society) in San Francisco and becomes its chairman.

Dosan as student in America

1904

Twenty-six years old, he and his wife move to Riverside, California. He studies English and Christianity at a Bible Study Center and works as a "school boy" (domestic worker).
Feb 1904, the Russo-Japanese War begins.

1905

His first son, Philip Ahn, is born in Highland Park, near Los Angeles. (March 28) The Korean Friendship Society is reorganized into the Kong Nip Hyup Hoe (Mutual Independence Association) the first politically oriented Korean

Helen Ahn and her son Philip Ahn

organization outside of Korea, and Dosan becomes its first chairman. (April 5) He establishes an office for the Kong Nip Hyup Hoe on Pacific Street in San Francisco. (Nov 14) He publishes the first issue of Kong Nip Shin Bo (Newspaper). (Nov 20) On September 5 the Treaty of Portsmouth is signed. The Russo-Japanese War ends. Japan defeats Russia. On November 17, Eul Sa Jo Yak - Protectorate Agreement of 1905 was signed, whereby Japan took over the control of Korea's Foreign Affairs Department.

1906

April 18, the Kong Nip Hyup Hoe office on Pacific Street burns down due to the San Francisco earthquake, and Dosan temporarily moves his office across the Bay to

Founding member of Kong Nip Association (Dosan at right)

Oakland. Imperial Japan sets up the Governor General's Office to rule Korea and Ito Hirobumi is appointed as its first governor.

1907

January 8 Twenty-nine years old, he leaves for Korea from San Francisco to find out the extent of Japan's control of Korea.

February His boat stops in Japan. He makes a speech about patriotism to Tae Geuk Hak Hoe, a Korean student group in Tokyo.

February 20 He arrives in Korea.

April He establishes a secret society, ShinMinHoe (the New People's Association), consisting of Lee Dong-Nyung, Lee Shi-Young, Ahn Tae-Guk, Lee Seung-Hoon, Kim Ku, Shin Chae-Ho and other prominent patriots. Dosan serves as the judge for the new incoming members.

May 12 He makes a speech about world powers, explaining their policies and plans, and asserts that Korea should prepare for war.

May 20 He discusses Korea's future with members of Tae Geuk Hak Hoe in Tokyo.

June He makes a speech about improving houses and construction of model farms.

July 8 He makes a speech about the importance of education for girls at an

Kong Nip Association building as it looks today

Kong Nip Shinbo (Newspaper)

Korea Daily News published by Shin Min Hoe

event at Myung Ryun Dang sponsored by Pyongyang Research Society for Women's Education.

August 1 Imperial Japan dissolves the Korean army. Korean troops resist, and Japanese soldiers open fire near Seoul Station. Dosan rescues and treats the wounded Korean soldiers and gets them to Severance Hospital.

October He discusses plans for activities in the Far East, with Yi Gang.

November He has a meeting with Governor General Ito Hirobumi. He declines Ito's proposal to form a cabinet to rule Korea together.

1908

January He establishes Northwest Students Society, the first youth movement organization in Korea.

March He tours Korea and makes plans with his colleagues for ShinMinHoe.

March 23 Jang In-Hwan and Jeon Myung-Woon assassinate Durham Stevens, foreign affairs advisor to the Japanese Governor General, in San Francisco. Stevens was campaigning in the United States for Japanese control of Korea.

September 26 He opens the Dae Sung School in Pyongyang. He installs Yoon Chi-ho as its principal, and takes a supporting role for himself.

September He forms Masan Ceramics Company along with

Lee Deok-Hwan and Kim Nam-Ho, funders for this venture in Pyongyang. He establishes Tae Geuk publishing company and book stores in Pyongyang, Seoul, and Daegu, with Ahn Tae-Guk in charge of the operation.

October 2 He initiates Asia Industries, Inc. to support the independence movement in the Far East region. The company name later was changed to Tae Dong Industries, Inc.

Stock certificates for Tae Dong Industries, Inc.

1909

January 14 He makes a speech entitled, "Future and Hope," at the Seoul YMCA.

February 3 He instructs Dae Sung students to refuse to wave Japanese flags when Korean King Soonjong tours the area.

Tae Sung School teachers and students, 1909

August He initiates the youth movement by establishing the Young Students Society sponsored by the ShinMinHoe.

October 26 Ahn Joong-Geun assassinates Governor General Ito

Site of Ito shooting by Ahn Joong-geun

Hirobumi at a railway station in Harbin, China.

October 31 Dosan is arrested for conspiring to assassinate Ito Hirobumi with Ahn Joong-Geun. He is incarcerated in Young Deung Po prison.

December 31 Dosan is released from prison after two months.

1910

March He conducts an emergency meeting with officers of the Shin MinHoe, which adopts 'Independence War' as the priority strategy to save the nation from Japan and decides

Annexation document

to develop military bases outside Korea for the independence fighters, as well as to establish military schools.

July He arrives in Tsing Tao, China and discusses future independence movement plans with Yi Gap, Yoo Dong-yol, and Kim Hee-sun. He composes "Ganda, Ganda, Ganda" a song about leaving Korea.

August 24 He arrives in Vladivostok and begins independence work with Koreans in Russia.

August 29 Day of shame. Japan officially annexes Korea. Koreans

"Farewell Korea" song by Dosan

have no country of their own. The Korean Young Students Association is terminated by the Japanese.

December 18 He forms a committee to initiate a youth group in Siberia

1911

January 2 He discusses with Koreans in Russia about the establishment of a school. He teaches history at a night school and makes a speech about patriotism.

February 7 He tours Mishansien in northern Manchuria for possible sites for a military school and returns to Vladivostok.

March 6 He holds a meeting with representatives of youth groups in Vladivostok.

August 24 He arrives in London via train having traveled from northern Manchuria to St. Petersburg and Berlin.

September 2 He arrives in New York and is processed through Ellis Island.

September 26 He arrives in Sacramento and visits a farm run by Koreans.

September 28 He arrives in San Francisco and gives a speech at a welcoming event.

November He tours Korean communities in California.

1912

January 29 With Song Chong-Ik and Lim Jung-Ki, he

establishes North American Industrial Company, Inc. with capital of $45,000.

July 5 His second son, Philson, is born in Riverside.

November 8 through 29 He organizes the Central Congress for the Korean National Association and becomes its first chairman.

Korean National Association building

Korean National Association members

1913

May 12 He makes a speech in San Francisco about the responsibility of the Korean community with respect to the closing of Shin Han Minbo due to lack of funds.

May 13 In San Francisco, he forms the Hungsadan (Young

Hungsadan magazine, *We Build Today for Tomorrow*

Korean Academy), an organization of the young elites as a core to revive the spirit of the nationalist movement. Founding members are from all eight provinces of Korea.

July 2 In response to the Hemet Incident where Koreans were attacked by local residents, who mistook them for Japanese, the KNA (Korean National Association) receives assurances from the U.S. Department of the State and William Jennings Bryan that no affairs concerning Koreans will be handled through the Japanese consulate. He re-establishes the Claremont Students Center and speaks about the future of Koreans.

Dosan with teachers of Clairmont Student Center

1914

Dosan's family moves from Riverside to Los Angeles.

April 6 The Korean National Association, North American Branch, receives cor-porate status from the California state government.

July 28 World War I begins.

July to August He visits all Korean communities in California.

August 9 He gives a speech entitled "The Happiness of

Korean National Association registration document

Mankind" at a Korean church in San Francisco.

August 12 He gives a speech entitled "Our Time for Preparation" at a Korean church in San Francisco.

1915

January 16 Susan Ahn, Dosan's first daughter, is born in Los Angeles.

February He is re-elected as the chairman of the Central Congress of the Korean National Association.

Author with Susan Ahn and her son Philip Cuddy

June 23 He gives the inaugural speech as the chairman of the Central Congress of the KNA.

August 31 He arrives in Hawaii to resolve an argument about the leadership of the independence movement in Hawaii between Syngman Rhee and Park Yong-Mahn of the KNA.

Korean National Association building in LA, 2010

September 13 He gives a speech in Hawaii at the Fort Street Theater about patriotism and Korean spirit.

Dosan with officers of Korean National Association, Hawaii

October, November He visits all the islands and all the Korean communities in Hawaii to revive their motivation to support the independence movement and the KNA.

December He departs Hawaii for San Francisco.

1916

February He gives a speech at the Los Angeles branch of the KNA regarding "Next Step in the Evolution of Our People."

April 27 He gives speech in support of establishing Korean language school for children at Claremont Student Center.

1917

January 10 North America Industries, Inc. is established at the Hungsadan headquarters.

May 27 Dosan's second daughter Soorah is born in Los Angeles.

August 25 He opens a Korean language school for children at the Claremont Student Center.

Dosan with members of Korean National Association, Mexico

October 17 He visits Mexico and gives a speech about the tasks that lie ahead for Koreans in Mexico. He consolidates the Korean communities in Mexico and initiates a new contract between ranchers and Korean laborers. He visits Cuba and organizes KNA branch there.

April 23 He relays the conditions of Koreans in Mexico to the *Shin Han Minbo* (The New Korea) newspaper.

May 29 He departs Mexico for Los Angeles.

August 29 He Arrives in Los Angeles.

October 9 He gives a speech entitled, "Our Unfortunate Koreans Have No Pleasure" at the Los Angeles branch of the KNA.

October He presents a paper entitled, "The End of WWI and Our Tasks Ahead."

November 1 He issues a letter to all Koreans in North America, Hawaii, and Mexico calling for unity.

November 11 World War I ends.

November 25 He organizes a meeting of North American KNA branches to decide about sending Korean representatives to the Paris Peace Conference and the Small Nations Alliance Conference.

December 23 He calls a meeting of all the KNA branches and discusses the Korean situation.

1919

March 1 In Korea, the March 1 Movement begins.

March 9 He convenes an emergency

Susan and Soorah, 1919

March 1 Declaration of Independence

meeting of the KNA and decides to support a Declaration of Independence.

March 13 He is elected as the representative of the KNA at a general meeting. He makes a speech entitled, "Let's Support the 3.1 Movement," urging Koreans in America to provide economic support.

March 17 The KNA decides to dispatch special committee members to all of its branches in North America, Hawaii, and Mexico.

March 29 He sends a telegram to all of the participating countries at the Paris Peace Conference, expressing the absolute necessity for independence of Korea, and requests permission for Kim Kyu-shik's attendance at the conference.

April 1 He departs San Francisco with $6,000 raised for the purpose of establishing the Korean Provisional Government (KPG) in Shanghai.

Korea Provisional Government,
Shanghai

Dosan as Interim Prime
Minister, 1919

May 25 He arrives in Shanghai via Honolulu and Hong Kong.

June 4 He gives a speech concerning ways to advance the independence movement at a church in Shanghai.

June 28 He is selected as the Minister of the Interior as well as acting Prime Minister for KPG in Shanghai.

July 8 He issues Republic of Korea Treasury bonds in the name of the Minister of the Interior. He establishes a poll tax system. He reports to the KPG assembly regarding the direction of the foreign affairs department and its intent to focus on diplomatic activities in Washington D.C. and Paris.

July 10 The KPG issues its first directive, announcing its

Korea Provisional Government bond

secret communication system.
It decides to consolidate the
KPG and the Korean National
Association of America.

Founding Korean Red Cross

July 13 He establishes, in the
name of the Minister of the
Interior, the Korean Red Cross.

July 17 He is appointed chairman
of the KPG historical archive
committee.

Publication material by
Korea Provisional Govt.

August 21 He begins publication
of "*Independence (Tong Nip)*," the
official newspaper of the KPG, later
renamed as "*Independence Newspaper (Tong Nip Shin Mun)*"
beginning September 25.

September 2 A public relations committee is established under

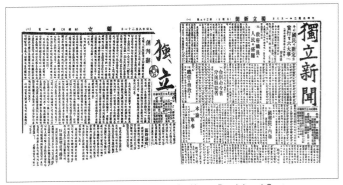

The *Independent* newspaper by Korea Provisional Govt.

the Ministry of the Interior.

September 6 The assembly enacts a new constitution regarding the governing structure of KPG.

September 28 He presents a revised constitution and a revised plan for the KPG to the cabinet.

December 7 He gives a speech entitled, "Let's Not Deviate [from our mission] "in Shanghai.

1920

January 3 He proposes "Six main tasks we must achieve," including military, education, diplomacy, judiciary, treasury, and unification, and details for each item.

January 19 He is elected as the chair of the Propaganda Bureau.

February 8 He participates in a military research committee and organizes the military research bureau.

February 14 He resigns his posts, faced by criticisms of "practicing provincialism and for his political ambition." The Far East Committee of the Hungsadan conducts membership installation ceremony for the first time in Shanghai.

March 1 He makes a speech as the Minister of Labor at the 3.1 memorial service. He calls for an end to the internal strife and for Koreans to focus their energy on their fight against Imperial Japan.

March 10 He is appointed as the Minister of Propaganda and takes on the duties of the Propaganda Bureau.

March 20 The KPG institutes an army draft system and begins a draft registration drive.

April 24 He discusses future plans for resolving factionalism with Yi Dong-whi, Lee Dong-nyung, and Lee Shi-young.

May 7 The KPG establishes the post of general commander for the Korea Liberation Army.

May 17 He establishes a temporary housing system by dispatching representatives to North Gando, Noryung, and South Gando [in Manchuria].

August 15 He meets with a team of American congressmen in Beijing. He requests American support for KPG's struggle against the Japanese Annexation and occupation of Korea. He meets Stephen G. Porter, the Chairman of the House Foreign Relations Committee.

September 3 He gives a speech in Mo A Dang in Shanghai about the Pacific Conference. Dosan criticizes the path adopted by the proponents of a "diplomatic solution."

Dosan with founding members, Hungsadan, Fareast Branch

[The Pacific Conference was proposed by Warren G. Harding to be held in Washington, D.C. to discuss the reduction of arms in the Pacific region, with Britain, France, Italy, and Japan. Many in the KPG thought — following lackluster interest in Korea at the Paris Peace Conference — that the Pacific Conference in Washington, D.C. was a good forum for the world powers to take up the Korean question, considering the cooling relationship between Japan and the U.S. at the time. Syngman Rhee, a proponent of gaining independence through diplomacy, needed a cause he could work on in order to maintain his position at the KPG, and became interested in the Pacific Conference, assigning himself as the head of the delegation to the Pacific Conference.]

September Dosan establishes the Far East branch of the Hungsadan in Shanghai, which takes in China, Russia, Korea, and Japan.

November 27 He gives a speech about forming the Great Independence Party.

December 21 He is the opening speaker at a speech rally to help Koreans in North Gando where Japanese soldiers had locked Koreans in a church and burned them to death.

December 29 He holds the Far East Hungsadan branch 7th annual Hungsadan convention held in Shanghai for the first time. Previously, it was only held in San Francisco and Los Angeles by the local branches.

February 27 Lee Dong-nyung, Lee Shi-young, Shin Ik-hee refuse to accept the post of KPG Prime Minister.

May 11 He resigns his post as Minister of Labor.

May 12 He and Yeo Woon-hyung are the opening speakers at a speech rally at Sang Hyun Dang in Shanghai, requesting formation of Kuk Min Dae Pyo Hoe Ui (the Assembly of Representatives) and organize an action committee to pursue the Assembly of Representatives.

Dosan with members of Korean Provisional Govt., 1921

May 29 Ad hoc committee for the Assembly of Representatives is formed.

July 7 He sends "Letter for My Comrades" to Hungsadan members in North America, Hawaii, and Mexico.

September 1 He gives a speech at the meeting called by supporters of the Pacific Conference.

September 14 He applies for an American visa, but the application is denied.

November He serves as the
principal of In Sung School in
Shanghai for nine months.

Dosan at an Insung School outing

January 23 He is appointed
as the president of Tong Ui Gun, an independence army in
Manchuria.

February 12 Su Yang Dong Mang Hoe (the Character
Cultivation Alliance) is formed at Yi Kwang- su's home in
Seoul.

June 6 He is elected as the acting chairman of the first
convention of the action committee for the Assembly of
Representatives.

June 16 KPG decides on a "vote of no confidence" against
Syngman Rhee leading to his impeachment.

July He organizes the Si Sa Chaik Jin Hoe (Current Affairs
Truth Commission) designed to resolve the differences in
ideas concerning the independence movement, attended by
30 individuals including Ahn Chang-Ho, Lee Dong-nyung,
Yeo Woon-young, Kim Ku, Cha I-seok. Dosan is elected as its
chairman.

August 14 The Action Committee meeting for the Assembly of
Representatives opens.

November He participates in a study effort to compare and analyze ideas for revolution.

1923

January 3 The Assembly of
Representatives is formed,
and holds its first session. 200

Candidate site for Ideal Village in
Jilin

leaders from 70 organizations attend.

January 18 He is elected as Vice Chair of the Assembly of
Representatives.

May 15 The Assembly of Representatives is dissolved after 63
sessions.

December He starts touring Manchuria to check on potential
sites for the "Ideal Village," a developmental model community
for the independence movement.

1924

January He continues his
tour in Manchuria to locate
potential sites for the "Ideal
Village."

February He presents
a paper in Shanghai
concerning unification and

Dosan with Dong Myung Academy
teachers

initiates the unification movement of nationalists, communists,
anarchists. He hopes to unify ideologies and strategies under

one independence movement.

March 3 He opens Dong Myung School in Nanjing, supported by the Hungsadan in America.

April 8 He meets Yi Kwang-su in Beijing and agrees to adopt the Character Cultivation Alliance as a part of the Hungsadan, Far East branch, and discusses publishing a magazine.

October 30 The 4th Hungsadan Far East convention is held in Nanjing.

November 22 He departs for Hawaii.

Dosan with Koreans in Hawaii, 1924

December 16 He arrives in San Francisco.

1925

January 20 He writes a letter to Lee Yu-pil and Cho Sangsup, recommending Park Eun-shik and Lee Sang-ryong as transitional heads of the KPG.

January 23 He writes a series of articles, "Letter to My Fellow Countrymen" in Dong A Ilbo in Korea. His writing is stopped by the Japanese Governor General.

March 23 The KPG Congress impeaches Syngman Rhee and elects Park Eun-shik as president.

April–July He tours Korean communities in the eastern United States – New York, New Haven, Boston and Philadelphia.

May 22 He visits Philip Jaisohn (aka Suh Jae-pil) in Philadelphia.

Dosan's writing, "For My Countrymen"

June 17 He gives a speech entitled "Our Ideological Spirit and Its Fulfilment" to the Korean Students Association convention in Chicago.

June–July He tours the Salt Lake City area with Jang Ri-wook to gather information on how the Mormon Church manages its community. The information was gathered for use with the establishment of a base for independence work.

August–November He tours Korean rice farms in Northern California.

Dosan with Chang Ri-wook

1926

February 26 He departs San Pedro for Shanghai. This is the last time Dosan's children will ever see him. Helen Ahn sees him in San Francisco a few days later because the boat (the S.S. Sonoma) broke down and docked for repairs.

March 8 He gives a speech at a church in Hawaii in commemoration of the 7th anniversary of the March 1st Movement.

March 13 He writes Helen Ahn a letter informing her he had to leave Hawaii under the orders of the U.S. immigration officials and would make an unplanned trip to Australia via American Samoa and Fiji.

March 23 He arrives in Sydney, Australia and gathers information on developing raw land.

April 14 He departs Sydney for China.

May 8 The KPG appoints Dosan as head of its State Department while he is absent.

May 16 He arrives in Shanghai and declines the appointment.

May 20 He publishes *Dong Gwang* magazine. He contributes articles written under a penname, San Ong. (He wrote "Unity and Division," May, 1926; "Are You an Owner?" June, 1926; "Heartless Society and Compassionate Society," June, 1926; Leader— Requisite for Unity," August, 1926; "From Artificiality

Dosan's writing in *Dong Gwang* magazine

to Conscientiousness," September, 1926; "Korean Students Today," December, 1926, among others.)

June 10 The Mansei (Long Live) Korea movement takes place, as a follow-up to the 3.1 Movement. On this day of the funeral for the last king of Joson, Soon Jong, about 24,000 people gather around the Jongno area in Seoul and shout "Mansei" as his procession passes by. This is referred to as the 6.10 Mansei Movement.

July 8 Dosan gives the opening speech for a rally at Samil Dang in Shanghai on the subject of "The Existence of the Korean Provisional Government and the Great Revolutionary Party."

July 19 A financial support group for KPG holds a general meeting at Samil Dang.

September 11 He lectures on the necessity of forming Yu (exclusive) Il (one) TongNip (independence) Party.

September 26 His third son Pil-young is born in Los Angeles.

October 16 He establishes a support group in Beijing for forming the Great Independence Party.

December He leaves for Manchuria to continue to seek potential sites for his "Ideal Village" program.

1927

January 27 He lectures on "Joseon Independence Movement, Past and Present" in Jilin. He is arrested by the Japanese during the lecture, but released in 20 days.

News article on Dosan's
activities in Jilin

Dosan with Yu Il Party
members

February He lectures all over Manchuria and urges "great
unity."

March 21 He forms a support group for the One Korea
Independence Party in Shanghai.

April 1 A farmer's organization (Nong Min Ho Jo Sa) to
support the welfare of Manchurian farmers is established.

May 8 He establishes a support group for the One Korea
Independence Party in Gwangdong.

July He establishes a support group for the One Korea
Independence Party in Muhan.

August 1 *Dong Gwang* magazine suspends publication after 16
issues.

September 27 A support group for the One Korea
Independence Party is formed in Nanjing.

November Support groups for the One Korea Independence
Party form a federation in Shanghai.

1928

May 20 He strongly calls for the cooperation of China and Korea in his editorial in a Chinese newspaper called *Se Gye* and a Korean newspaper the *Joong Ang Ilbo*.

May He establish a support group in Jilin, Manchuria for One Korea Independence Party.

December 20 He speaks to the Yon Hee School soccer team: "an individual gives himself to the nation, thereby completing his duties to himself and his duties to mankind." He proposes the idea of Dae (Great) Gong (Republic) Ju Ui (ism).

1929

February 8 He writes to Hungsadan members in America, clarifying that the Hungsadan is not an organization for character cultivation, but an organization for training leaders for the revolution.

February He visits the Philippine Islands and establishes a Korean Nation Association branch.

March 30 He returns to China.

October 26 The support group for One Independence Party of Shanghai is dissolved.

November He combines all the entities that agree with the principles of One Independence Party and initiates the forming of the Korean Independence Party.

1930

January The Hungsadan Far East branch holds its 6th annual convention.

January 25 The Korean Independence Party is formed by 25 nationalists who support Dae Gong Ju Ui (Great Republic).

February The KPG opposes forming the Korean Independence Party. The Party is dissolved.

April 5 He invites representatives from all the entities involved in independence work to a meeting in Chun Jin in June.

June 15 The Korean Great Independence Party issues *Joseon ji Hyeol* (Blood of Joson) magazine.

December Plans for Dong In Ho Jo Sa, a financial partnership with Hungsadan members, are announced.

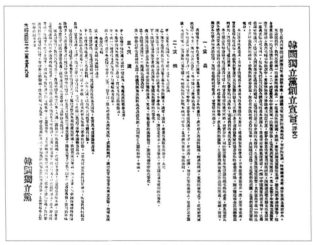

Declaration for Korea Independence Party

1931

January The Hungsadan Far East holds its 7th annual convention.

January 1 *Dong Gwang* magazine resumes publication.

February He contributes an article to *Dong Gwang* Magazine entitled, "My Pleading with Youth: About Character Building, Training as a Unit."

March 25 Dong In Ho Jo Sa (Mutual Cooperative Organization) is renamed Gong Pyong Sa (Fair Practice Organization), and holds a general meeting at the Hungsadan headquarters.

May 11 He attends the Kung Min party convention and begins to lobby for Korean representation in Manchuria.

July 18 The Coalition of Korean entities is formed to negotiate with Chinese authorities more effectively.

October 27 Dosan invites Chinese representatives to discuss forming a Korea-China coalition to fight against Imperial Japan.

November He meets with Chinese Kung Min Party member Wang Jung Wi and discusses organizing the 'United Front Alliance against Japan' together.

1932

January 8 Lee Bong-chang attempts to kill the Japanese Emperor Hirohito in Tokyo with a bomb, but he fails and is arrested.

January 18 The Hungsadan Far East holds its 8th annual convention in Shanghai.

April 29 Yoon Bong-gil assassinates a Japanese general in a bombing in Shanghai at Hongkew Park. Dosan is arrested by French police and turned over to the Japanese authorities.

Patriot Yoon Bong-gil

May 30 Dosan is transferred to a Japanese prison in Incheon, Korea.

June 2 A group is formed in Shanghai to free Dosan.

June 7 He is transferred to Seoul.

July 25 He is found guilty of violating the 'Peace Preservation Law' and incarcerated in Seo Dae Mun prison in Seoul.

December 19 The Japanese court in Seoul sentences him to a 4-year prison term.

Dosan arrested, 1932

1933

He gives up his appeal, and is transferred to Dae Jon prison.

Dosan's letter to his family, 1933

1934

He continues to serve his prison term in Dae Jon prison.

1935

February 10 He is released from Dae Jon prison and stays with Park Heung-shik in Seoul.

February 11 He arrives in Pyongyang and stays with Kim Dong-won.

February 14 He gives a sermon at Ki Yang Church in his hometown.

February 16 He leaves for Seoul.

February He tours all over Korea and afterwards he builds a retreat called Song Tae San Jang in Dae Bo Mountain in Pyong Nam province and takes up residence in the mountains.

Interior of Seo Dae Moon prison

Dosan after release with Yeo Woon-hyung (left) and Cho Man-sik (right)

Song Tae mountain residence

September 5 He is invited by the Andong Youth Organization to give a lecture to an audience of about 2,000. He speaks to them about manpower development and Dae Gong-ism (The

Great Republic concept).

November 13 A welcoming ceremony is planned for Dosan in Pyongyang, but halted by Japanese police.

Dosan with Shin Yoon-sik, Yi Kwang-su, et al

1936

February 20 He leaves for Seoul to tour the southern provinces.
February 30 He arrives at Seoul.
August He sends a telegram to Sohn Ki-jung to congratulate him for winning the gold medal for the Marathon at the Berlin Olympics.

Dosan with colleagues, 1936

1937

June 28 He is accused of holding secret meetings and is arrested along with Dong Woo Hoe (Friendship Society) members. 150 people are arrested. The Japanese declare the Dong Woo Hoe is the same type of organization as the Hungsadan and accuse members of violating the "Peace Preservation Law".

Dosan with colleagues, 1937

August 10 He is incarcerated at
Jongno police station.

November 1 He is transferred to Seo
Dae Mun prison.

December 24 He is transferred to
Keijo Hospital (now Seoul National
University hospital) due to his severe
illnesses. He had been arrested
more than five times over his years
of independence work. His health had deteriorated with
each arrest and the following imprisonments and torture. He
suffered from tuberculosis, a common ailment in Korea at the
time, compounded by Plevritis and peritonitis.

Dosan in prison, 1937

1938

January Dong Woo Hoe members,
42 of them, are found guilty of
violating "Peace Preservation Law."

March 10 He dies in the hospital.

March 12 He is buried in Mang
Woo Ri public cemetery.

March 13 Leftist groups hold a
memorial service for Dosan in
Hangu, China.

Reporting of Dosan's death

March 13 The Korean National Association of Hawaii holds a

Memorial service for Dosan in Los Angeles

memorial service for Dosan.

March 22 A memorial service is held in Los Angeles.

April 10 A memorial service is held in Chung Jing, China.

Ralph (Pil Young), Philip, Susan Ahn in service during WWII, 1944

1947

March 10 The Dosan Ahn Chang-Ho Memorial Foundation is established in Korea.

Kim Ku's writing honoring Dosan

Syngman Rhee's writing honoring Dosan

1948

The Hungsadan headquarters is moved from Los Angeles to Seoul.

Hungsadan headquarters building, 2011

1962

March 1 He is honored by the South Korean government with a Presidential Medal for his contribution to nation building.

1963

Lee Hye Ryon (Helen Ahn) makes her first visit to Korea since she left for America with Dosan in 1902.

1969

April 21 Lee Hye-ryon dies in Los Angeles.

President Park Chung-hee greeting Helen Ahn

1971

April 6 Construction of Dosan Park begins at Shin Sa-dong in Gang Nam-ku, Seoul.

1972

August 22 The Dosan Ahn Chang-Ho Memorial Foundation is resurrected.

1973

November 10 The remains of Dosan and Lee Hye-ryon are interred together during the opening day dedication ceremony at Dosan Park.

Gravesite for Dosan and Helen Ahn

1985

March 9 The Dosan Thoughts Study Center (renamed the Dosan Scholar Association) is established.

1997

December 23 Construction of Dosan Ahn Chang-Ho Memorial Hall begins.

Ground breaking ceremony for Dosan Memorial Hall

1998

November 9 Dosan Ahn Chang-Ho Memorial Hall opens.

Opening ceremony for Dosan Memorial Hall

Dosan Memorial Hall

Dosan Memorial exhibition hall

Dosan's Writings on Leadership

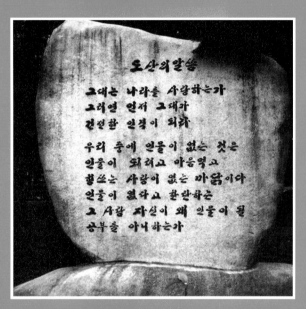

Dosan's writing carved in stone.

Do you love your country?
Then, first, you become a wholesome person.
The reason we do not have leaders among us is
because we do not train to be leaders.
There are people who lament that we have no leaders.
Why don't they try to be leaders themselves?

1

Prerequisite to Unity: Leadership

Dong Gwang magazine, August 1926

If we are going to work together on a common mission, have trust and cooperate with each other, we must have a leader. If we left everything we do to our own devices, we would only do things in this world for our own benefit. Even though we may ask a good leader for his advice, we would turn it down because we say it is unnecessary. In the world of cooperation, whether we engage in a small cooperative task or a big one, there must be an overall leader in order to carry out the task and achieve the objective. On the contrary, if we do not have a leader, we will not actually realize the cooperative effort, nor will we gain its results.

Let us consider a musical band. Aside from a solo performance with a horn or piano, an orchestra with a drum, horn, clarinet, or *geo mun goh* (Korean harp) trying to play together in harmony follows a conductor who leads the whole orchestra. This is not just to give someone the title of leader; a conductor is mandatory for making music together. That is not all. If you are going on a tour with a group of people, sometimes you need a leader for the tour group, not just in name, but in reality. In addition, the military, police, business groups, teachers' group, political parties, research groups....every cooperative effort known to mankind has designated leaders. A project of minor scale gets a minor leader; and a project of major scale gets a major leader.

I ask all of you — can't you see? A nation of people, no matter how they are organized, to whatever ideology they subscribe, there is always a leader. Even those people who reject nationalism in favor of so-called globalism, they have a leader, too.

Everyone! Did we establish a leader, or did we not? Some of our brothers and sisters who read this, may say, 'How elementary, how useless, everyone knows this.' After looking at our society, I am not sure how many people actually know that we need a leader. Young people of today insist on equality, and they seem to think that it would be an insult for them to have a leader over them. I keep telling everyone, "Let's unite, let's unite," but it is hard to meet anyone who is interested in, or concerned about, finding a leader who can unite us.

Is There a Leader or Not?

We understand the need for leaders, of course. But then the next question is whether we have the people to select as leaders. I hear many people say that there is nobody qualified to become a leader, and that it is impossible to select a leader no matter how much we try and that we should wait until more qualified people come along.

Is this right?

I don't think so.

If we say there is no qualified leader today, there will never be one in a hundred or a thousand years. If we say there will be a qualified leader in a thousand years, there is one today. Those who say there is no qualified leader today do not understand what leaders do.

How do we recognize a qualified leader?

Whatever the cooperative effort is, someone who is ahead of others is the leader of that group. In other words, the qualification to be a leader is a relative thing. We are not here to compare one individual to another. We need to look at the cooperative effort itself, and compare those who are involved in the cooperative effort, and determine who is ahead of everyone else and recognize him as the leader.

A Leader Is Here for Certain

Earlier, I made a reference to an orchestra. There are various types of orchestras, some are good, and some are bad. A superb orchestra has a top class conductor, and an orchestra of marginal quality has an inferior conductor. If we compare the two conductors, we can say that the second conductor is not qualified to be a conductor, yet he is the most advanced among the members of his orchestra, therefore, we should say that he is a qualified conductor for that orchestra. This is true for other areas. A cooperative effort with highly intelligent scholars is led by someone who is the most capable of the other scholars, and a cooperative effort with uneducated laborers is led by someone just as uneducated as the others, but a little ahead of the group.

It is a different story if we are not involved in any kind of cooperative effort. But once we are engaged in a cooperative effort, we must have a leader to help us achieve our goal. When we select our leader, we should not compare our leader with those of the other groups, but we should make comparisons within our own group. That is the fundamental principle for all human societies, isn't that so? When we look at our own society, such as it is, we are sure to have a qualified leader, someone who is more advanced than the rest of us. In the future when our character improves, we will have a leader of higher caliber. So, I say to you, we will always have a qualified leader no matter what. So, saying that we have no leader just means we do not understand the truth about cooperative efforts. And that is why we do not put up a leader.

Great Heart, Path to Greatness

Think about it, everyone! Do we think that in our land everyone is equally sincere and equally capable, with no one who goes ahead of us or behind us? That is not possible. When I look over my fatherland with my own eyes, I can see great people who are qualified to lead us. When I see them, I put them up as our leaders, with love and respect.

You can see what I am saying. A great man is nothing special. A great man is someone who does great things with the heart of a great man. Whether he is recognized or not, he devotes his wealth, knowledge, time, and passion for our people, even though he is the target of hatred and oppression. These people are doing great things with the heart of great people and they are very qualified to be our leaders. Are they among us? They are. I can see them, and so do you. They are ahead of us in their sincerity and ability; therefore, how can we say we have no qualified leaders?

Discard Jealousy

I don't know if my assessment is correct or not, but absence of qualified people is not the reason why we don't have a leader. There may be myriad other reasons for not having a leader, but the main reason we don't have a leader is simply because of our jealousy, our greatest enemy. We are afraid to appoint a leader, never mind helping him and much less supporting him. We try to topple a qualified person to prevent him from becoming a leader.

The saddest example in our history is Admiral Yi Soon-shin. From 1545 to 1598, he led the Korean navy to battle, demolishing the invading Japanese armada. He was the leader Koreans should have selected and supported, but our jealous ancestors plotted against him and toppled him. More recently, we had a great man like Yu Gil-joon [1856–1914, Reformist, Politician] who had substantial qualifications to become our leader; unfortunately our predecessors persecuted him and ignored him until he died. Then they gave him an elaborate funeral, which made me even sadder.

We will not get ourselves on the right path to the true national movement until this situation is remedied someday.

Do Good Work; Get Blamed

Everyone! We keep silent about those wealthy people in our community, who do not spend their money for our [independence] cause, even those who spend money to harm us. Yet those who spend their money for our people are criticized and persecuted. Small funders of our cause are lightly persecuted and significant funders, severely persecuted [for causing troubles].

We keep silent about those people who have modern educations and do not use their knowledge for our cause; and, even about those who use their knowledge against our people. Yet we criticize and persecute those who contribute their knowledge for our people. Small contributors are lightly persecuted and big contributors, severely persecuted.

In other words, people without character or sincerity have no problem. But we criticize people of significance, sincere people. That seems to be the present case.

We attack and criticize whoever earns the trust of the people in the countryside, calling him the ringleader of a provincial mob. If anyone earns the trust of an organization or entity, all other segments of our community rise up and attack him, calling him the ringleader of a faction.

Somehow, we find ways to tear down and discredit any intelligent person who attracts the attention of young people.

Look here! Those who spend their money for the good of our people are ahead of those who do not. Those who contribute their knowledge, their time, and their passion are ahead of those who do not. Those who earn the trust of the folks in the countryside or of an organization are ahead of those who do not. Those who are adored by young people are ahead of those who are not.

Foolishly, we persist to drag down those who are ahead of us, as I said earlier, and we waste so much time and energy trying to prevent qualified people from becoming leaders.

When we look at our social trends today we consider it the worst shame to say "I respect and admire so and so" or "I am going to be someone's subordinate." We proceed to mask our true feelings about someone we really admire and we pretend we don't know him, just like the apostle Peter had denied knowing Jesus. And we do not come to the defense of a person when he is criticized. As a result, it seems that respect for people in general is disappearing in our society today. Instead, words containing insults and ignorance are prospering.

Don't Push Your Crime onto Others

When it comes to the topic of leaders, we don't feel like talking about it, nor do we wish to hear anything about it. Consequently, even those who agree that we need leaders hesitate to say what they think in public. That is because the discussion doesn't go anywhere; it is useless to talk about it. Also, they are afraid that the public will reject them, suspect them, by bringing up the subject of asking to be treated as leaders.

Alas! I may be overreacting, but I think we have now reached the point of no return on the question of leaders. We simply don't want them. Or, they say, "If they do the right things, of course we would support them. All they do is cheat and fight. That's why we don't support leaders."

But this argument does not make sense. Leaders are supposed to be ahead of others, but cheaters and fighters are already behind everyone, so they are not leaders to begin with.

Then people say, "Everyone cheats and fights." That is not true. There may be only a few, but there are people who honestly work for our people with their own money, knowledge, and talents, without cheating. Also, I know some people who appear to be ruffians just because they are constantly criticized under attack, but they do not retaliate despite all forms of persecution levied against them. They simply go on with their work calm and even.

That is my observations. If it turns out that everyone cheats and fights, the person who cheats and fights the least is the qualified leader. Why? It is because he is ahead of everyone in terms of character.

Get rid of your jealous attitude and search with cool objectivity for the real leader of our people, you will see who is ahead of us. Cool objectivity only comes after we attain the sense of responsibility and pride as the owners of our country.

The real owner of a home feels happy and honored without a hint of jealousy to have an outstanding family member in his household. Older brother, or younger brother, it doesn't matter to him, or even having an intelligent servant... he would be happy. He is happy because he is only thinking about what is good for his home. The head of household wants his house to be better than anyone else's. He feels happy when a good person comes along in his family and he loves and protects him. Likewise, we want to have a better society than any other country and we wish hard for good people to come along, and when they do, we should feel happy and admire them and support them to the end.

This Is How You Find Leaders

I am speaking too long, so I will shorten my talk and offer several reference materials for selecting leaders. I ask that you consult them and other materials better than this and use them to establish leaders.

1. Do not recognize anyone as a leader based on vanity. First, investigate his ideology, character, policies, and ability, and see that his ideology and character suit your personality, and make sure that his methods and abilities are better than yours or others. Only then should you recognize him as your leader. Examine his qualities not by rumors that go around but by looking

into his actual history and actions.

2. Once you recognize his ideology and character and find sincerity, then you hang on to him. Correct him if he makes any mistakes in his speech or work, but do not readily discard him. Ruining his life just because of mistakes he once made, or entirely rejecting the person just because of one or two faults is not a desirable thing to do. In the past they used the principle of *Il Bul Sal Yuk Tong* (lose one point if you miss one answer [in a test], but lose six points if you guess an answer). But now, we grade our colleagues by the harsh principle of *Yuk Tong Saeng Il Bul* (Deduct six points for every missed answer.)

3. When you select leaders you should discard the concepts, *Chin So Won Geun* (believing those who are close to us but rejecting those who are distant) and Ja Dang Pi Dang (member of my party or not). You should set your standard according to the will of the majority of the people, and determine his qualifications with a fair and honest mind.

2
From Artificiality to Conscientiousness

Dong Gwang magazine, September 1926

Artificiality is the reason for defeat; conscientiousness is the foundation for success. Is our society vain or sincere? In other words, are we a failure or a success? I want to ask this big question and talk big. A while back I read in a newspaper about this famous foreign scholar. After he toured around Korea, a reporter asked him "What do you think about Korea's future?" He didn't say too much, he simply replied, "Koreans should get away from artificiality and enter the world of conscientiousness."

A foreign visitor fresh off the boat was able to

spot our artificiality the first time he stepped on our land and that makes me think that our condition is in such bad shape. News from our fatherland says that the latest booming business is *Mi Du Chue In*. (Buying and selling rice futures with partial down payment, similar to buying stocks on margin, set up by Japanese traders to shrewdly round up Korean rice in Inchon harbor for exporting to Japan.)

Everyone admits that this is a shaky business, an unreliable venture headed for certain failure. But many people are lined up to gamble in this business, and this shows how vain and empty our society has turned. How about people in other businesses? They may have good intentions but their methods are no better than the *Mi Du Chue In* business.

Alas! Artificiality was rampant when we lost our country, yet we have not pulled ourselves out of that trap. We are not even thinking about pulling out of the trap.

Meticulous Planning

Conscientiousness means this: whatever project we do, we plan and organize ourselves early, based on the rules of cause and effect; figure out what to do, when to do it, and how to do it; define the results we want; remain steadfast in our mission; and stay on the course we set with vigor until we achieve what we set out to do.

To the contrary, artificial people ignore the principles of cause and effect; they do not spend time on planning and thinking about the project; they count on lucky odds that might happen one out of a thousand chances; they hurry around helter-skelter, here, there, without direction; right from the start they do not care if the project has real merit; they run around insincerely and perform empty ceremonies meant to flash their name for a one-time show.

If we understand the meaning of artificiality and conscientiousness as defined above, we can easily determine without long, theoretical discussions which one is the path to success and which one is the path to failure. Some say that the business of politics is not conducive to the analyses of a bookworm; politicians employ dark, ambitious, and disingenuous means to reach their goals; politicians feign their attentiveness to people, clamoring that politics must reflect the contemporary mentality of the people; and fabricate their policies to fit an artificial mentality, thereby encouraging artificiality in the process. We do not live in the time of *Su Ho Ji* (14th century Chinese novel satirizing corrupt society); we live in an era of academics. Therefore, in politics or any other business, we must approach an issue with an academic concept even though we may not have academic knowledge. So, it is not time to put a fortune teller on a pedestal and have him tell our fortune about our rice caper. It is time to invite a learned person, establish his leadership, and follow his lead. He may falter under extenuating circumstances and utilize the people's weaknesses and temporarily follow an untrustworthy path. This will be bad enough. But then, we cannot make artificiality our main business, can we?

I would like to divulge one by one all the factual details of the events here and abroad related to the artificiality of the past, the reason for our failure, but I will stop here. I just want to say in general that things like extortion, cheating, family quarrels, and most of the evil happenings in our society are caused by artificiality. Moreover, artificiality was responsible for blocking the road to mutual trust and cooperation among fellow Koreans, for blocking the road to orderly business dealings among fellow Koreans, and for causing us to lose credibility among foreigners. To repeat, we could never achieve real success by artificial means; we have defeated ourselves. That is why the foreign scholar first mentioned the word conscientiousness in his advice for us.

More Conscientiousness As the Situation Worsens

It is easy to think that we do not have the luxury to talk about conscientiousness or artificiality given our dire situation at this time. But I think that our dire situation calls for quicker remedial action, that is, we have to try to build a conscientious society as soon as possible in order to get ourselves out of the situation we are in. I believe we will succeed if we do our best, although I regret that I can't back up my belief with real evidence. But I still believe that you will see the path to success if you look ahead into the future with genuine concern, whether I say anything or not.

For our great task ahead, let us build a strong foundation with truth (*Jin*) and love (*Jeong*), not false (*Heo*) pretenses (*Wi*). I say once more; let us build a strong foundation for our great task ahead with truth and love, not false pretenses. *Heo* and *Wi* represent false foundation; *Jin* and *Jeong* are strong like a great boulder.

Endeavor to Unite in Your March

Our society may be mired in artificiality now, but that does not mean every individual in our society is in the same plight. There are people who respect conscientiousness. I know you, I talked to you. I know that you are adversely affected by what you see, but I implore you, stay strong! Use the corruption around you to strengthen your genuineness. Do not stop caring! Do not stand there alone in the wild and let out quiet sighs in disgust. Search for others who feel the same as you. Find those genuine people, unite with them in a genuine way, collaborate with them on genuine tasks [independence work], and ascertain genuine results not only in theory but in actuality. Even if you do all this, artificial people will not follow you, they might even interfere with you; for their artificial minds will not allow them to agree with your genuine work. Even so, I still believe that your adversaries will discard their artificial ways and join you in the end if you keep moving ahead on your conscientious path.

Some Troublesome Conditions

I am not an accomplished writer, and I have difficulty in expressing myself by writing. Furthermore, because of my situation [Japanese censure], I have to be careful in what I am writing, unable to express myself freely. I don't know your reaction to my writing, but my intent for this repetitive piece is to implore you to take the responsibility for the present and future — in perpetuity — of our society and people. I implore each one of you to march toward righteous, worthy goals as the qualified owner; to never despair, never stop, never stray from the true course, and continue to march steady and strong until you reach the destination despite the difficulties and hurdles. Let us march forth together with the spirit of love and mutual respect for one another, build harmony with common causes for all the factions, establish solid leadership, build trust for each other, and cooperate.

March forth with common causes, but do not base them on artificial principles, only truths. So, please, keep these thoughts in mind. You may think that this is a small, ordinary problem, but I think this is very important in our work and that is why I mention it again. I think that in our society, we need to experience some grand awakening beyond the ordinary. Only then, someone or I will speak louder and something significant will actually happen.

3
Are You an Owner?

Dong Gwang magazine, June 1926

I ask you, my fellow countrymen! How many of us consider ourselves owners of our country?

You might say all Koreans are owners of Korea. Why am I asking how many owners there are? True, all Koreans are owners of Korea in name, but we don't know how many of us actually behave like owners.

If there is no owner in every household, the house collapses, or someone else must manage the house instead. A nation of people is the same, and so is our society. Therefore, when we consider the future of our nation, we first need to figure out if there are owners among us and, if so, how many. I feel I need to ask each of you if you are a genuine owner of our society.

If you are not an owner, you are a guest… and how do we differentiate an owner from a guest? An owner voluntarily feels responsible for the society, and a guest does not. Sometimes we shed tears for our society, shout angry words, even put ourselves in dangerous situations, but we shouldn't mistake these actions for the actions of an owner. A guest passes by a house and sees a tragic happening. He could cry, shout angry words, or put himself in a dangerous situation to save lives. But he is not an owner, just an occasional guest, and he doesn't feel responsible for the house. The owners I am looking for are the people who feel a genuine responsibility for our nation. Genuine owners of our nation do not criticize, praise, feel jealousy, or feel sympathy for our nation. Their only concern is the recovery of our nation, and all the criticisms and praises, words of sympathy, are reserved for the passing guest.

The real owner of a house does not turn his back on the house, whether or not all the affairs are in order; he does not abandon his family whether his family members are good or bad; he stays with his house and does his best to maintain its integrity till the day he dies. The real owner of the house becomes more interested in the house when it falls into difficulties and eventually comes up with a solution.

Likewise, the real owner of a nation does not ignore his work for one minute, not even a second, whatever the crisis or misfortune his society is facing, whether his people are despicable and faltering, no matter how many times his work for his people fails. Whatever his intellectual capability, sufficient or not, he only thinks about the condition of his people and makes detailed plans to save his people from such travesty, and acts on his plans until the day he dies. He is the owner.

When I was in my fatherland, I saw many people who were briefly fired up with righteous indignation and worked for our society, but rarely saw workers who behaved like owners with a permanent sense of responsibility. And there were workers who, for the sake of their own honor and as a way to elevate their images, pretended like they were true devotees of our society, but they were not.

In my view, I think there are true workers now, although not too many. Success or failure of an effort for a house or a nation depends on the soundness of the plans and execution of such plans. But there must be owners of the house or the nation before there can be any plans or execution of such plans.

Ultimately, the fundamental problem with any society is with the presence or absence of owners. I ask you to look around you and see if there are real owners and how many. If you see many people who behave like owners, never mind, but if you see only a few, then you should first try to produce qualified owners before anything else. Regardless of what went on in the past, I think the time is ripe for owners to stand up. I believe we are headed for self-realization.

4

Heartless Society, Compassionate Community: Meaning of Fellowship and Its Essence

Dong Gwang magazine, June 1926

Meaning of Fellowship

Fellowship (*Jeong Ui*) is made up of affection and sympathy. Affection means the warmth flowing out of a mother as she adores her child; sympathy means a mother's heart sharing the pain or joy of her child. (*Don Su*) means making *Jeong Ui* bigger, more, and thicker. In other words, I want to say that we should study affection and sympathy and do a good job making fellowship part of our lives.

Relationship between Fellowship and Society

Of all the humans, the most unfortunate are those who live in a heartless society, and the most fortunate are those who live in a compassionate society. Fellowship generates energy for a community; an energetic community is interesting, full of fun; and an interesting community is full of activities and courage.

A compassionate community is like a garden adorned with plenty of sun and rain, without any pain, only nurturing progress in all areas of human endeavor. A community filled with fun generates courage and prosperity, which lead to peace and happiness.

On the contrary, a heartless community is like a huge field of thorns thick with pain and suffering all around, and people come to hate the community in which they live. In other words, it is covered with dark clouds, pelted by cold wind and rain, filled with fear and gloom without any pleasure or fun. Thus the heartless community contracts, digresses, feels an endless oppression, generates no courage, has no activities, and becomes the enemy of the people in it, as the heartless community becomes saturated with pain and suffering.

Poor Korean Community

Our Korean community is heartless. I am sure that there are heartless communities in other countries, too, but our Korean community is the most unfortunate. This heartlessness brought the end of our nation. We lived for hundreds of years in a heartless society, thus we have the capacity to withstand the pain of a heartless society, and if people who are used to living in a compassionate society become part of a heartless society, they will probably dry up and die. We are now facing the problems of life and death, yet we are still very coldhearted. Our movement would have been more effective if our comrades practiced more fellowship. If we have fellowship, we have unity; thus there would be prosperity for our people.

Fellowship is a gift that originated in Heaven, and we, who embraced Confucianism, knew how to respect others, but we lost the art of loving others. And our traditions of honoring marriages, funerals, and ancestor worship have turned into empty ceremonies.

Truth about Our Heartless Society

Try to remember when you were a child. Love and affection between humans were natural occurrences; but in our society, we do not see any fellowship between parents and children, or between brothers.

Adults treat their children as their possessions, so they make the children cry or laugh just for their amusement. They tell the children frightening things like, "A tiger is coming," or "A ghost is coming," to tease them. And grandparents and parents in the house routinely admonish and punish young people, and the children cannot feel safe for a minute. Children shake with constant fear of a beating. When I was a child, I loved to play in the hills until late, and on the way home I was always afraid that I would get a beating. Sometimes, I was chased out of the house as a punishment for my mistakes. Even today, my heart aches when I see a child wandering about outside his home because his father kicked him out. Meanwhile, a mean school master awaits him at his school. But he goes to school because his parents make him go, not because he wants to.

Further, family members treat each other like enemies, parents and daughter-in-law, brothers, and what have you. Government officials are the same. Go and see what is going on at their local offices for villages, counties, and provinces. Every office is filled with a cold atmosphere. What is worse is the heartlessness between men and women. In our homes, if the husband and wife looked at each other and smiled or laughed, it would cause a near scandal. A man and woman couldn't even look at each other because of the lack of fellowship in our society. So, if a man and woman actually met and carried on a conversation, it would cause havoc in the community as if they were committing a crime. These conditions are hurdles in developing proper relations between men and women in our society.

Contents of a Compassionate Society

Let us now turn our attention to the compassionate society that exists somewhere else. Parents in their homes never become angry at their children. Parents give them dolls to teach them love and affection; they hug and kiss them when their children go to sleep. Children are treated well at the meal table. Parents do not yell at their children to eat their food. Consequently, children grow up in a warm environment without any fear. Children in the West are more precious than flowers. That is because they grow up in homes filled with love. When they go to school, most of the teachers in elementary schools are women. Women teachers have warmer hearts than men, and the children are very mindful of their teacher and they want to come to school. So, I have not seen any children refusing to go to school.

Not only school, but you can feel warm energy on ships and at meetings. People with worries do not push their problems onto others. Churches have an orchestra and a choir, and people gather and laugh together as they share meals, full of fellowship. Our churches are filled with fear. Love and affection arising out of our churches are not legitimate love; the congregation is forced to love because, if they do not, they fear they are committing a sin. In the West, they regard fellowship more highly than food or clothes. Merchants, students, and even newspaper boys belong to some club; they want to live surrounded by fellowship. One thing I envy most in America is the fact that everyone is happy and pleasant regardless of their position at work. When someone visits their house, they have their daughter or sister to greet you with smiles. Men and women engaged to be married hug each other expressing love. Nobody criticizes them for displaying affection in public, and they have no fear, only unbridled affection.

The union between a man and a woman is the basic ingredient for fellowship, but in our society, we keep them separated, making for a coldhearted environment. Westerners grow up in the world of fellowship, live out their lives surrounded by fellowship, and die in fellowship. Their fellowship generates energy, fun, and everything turns out well for them.

Let Us Learn How to Grow Fellowship

We cannot regard this fellowship business lightly. If we were to reform our society, we must first make it an affectionate one. Maybe we inherited heartless blood from our ancestors; traditionally we do not have warm affection. That is why we must study the subject of growing fellowship. Then, we can taste true living. Anyone who breathes one word, one act, to harm our fellowship is our enemy. Past or present, whenever our people gather, we assume that we would engage in a fight. Even if we criticize others, we shouldn't do it with thorny words; we should do it with love. Now here are a few things to remember in growing fellowship.

1. Do not meddle in someone else's business.

We often become presumptuous and get involved in someone else's business. We like digging for faults. We should pay attention to our own business, mend our own faults, and never get involved in matters concerning others.

2. Respect individuality. A sharp stone, or round stone, every stone is useful, so it is wrong to admonish others for having a different personality. We must respect individuality and accept that everyone has their way of doing things.

3. Do not invade the freedom of others. Every individual is entitled to his own freedom, even your comrades. Just because your comrade does not agree with you, it is silly to discard him as your comrade. Westerners ask their children, "Will you?" when they make a request out of respect for the children's freedom to decide.

4. Do not depend on your comrade for material help. Sometimes we ask our friends for money, and when they refuse, we become irate. So, it is better not to depend on our friends for material help. In the event that you requested help and received none, you shouldn't do anything to harm the fellowship.

5. Do not confuse fellowship. Father and son, husband and wife, friends, and comrades all have different kinds of fellowship. Is there any way that the father-son fellowship and the fellowship between friends are the same? And, there are closer comrades than others. So do not blame anyone for loving someone else.

6. Ascertain trust. Fellowship stays intact when you keep promises. If you do not do what you said you would, people become disappointed. So establishing trust is one of the conditions for growing fellowship.

Fellowship: Words to Live by

Patriotism comes in different shapes, depending on which society. A heartless society keeps digging for faults in a patriot, and when he runs into trouble, it doesn't help him. And, if someone contributes money to an endeavor and stops paying, people in a heartless society do not remember to thank him for all the money he has paid, but they chastise him for nonpayment. And a heartless society admonishes young people for following someone they respect. Where can you find a heartless society like that?

A compassionate society is different. If compassionate people, even older gentlemen or women, run across people in trouble along the road, they rush to help the needy. They do not differentiate the wealthy from the poor. They make bandages with their clothes and wrap the wounds and care for them.

Our people who live without fellowship are in painful hell. Korean society is a field of thorns. There is no pleasure. Let us build fellowship and live in warm energy. Let me repeat — there must be fellowship for warm energy to exist; there must be warm energy for fun and interest to exist; there must be fun and interest for success to exist. Only then, people become motivated to do whatever the work, whatever the duty. We should live our lives according to the words of fellowship.

5
Unity and Division
Dong Gwang May, 1926

When we look at our Korea today, we clamor we must unite, we must become one. But then why don't we unite? Why do we build walls and take sides? Why do we fight? Words of resentment and admonishment for each other fill the heaven and earth of Korea, and we get the feeling that we Koreans are not prone to unity but divisiveness. Yet, we Koreans appear to desire unity very badly. United, we prosper, divided, we go bankrupt. United, we live, divided, we die. We hear theories on unity in private and public places and we read about them in newspapers and magazines. Thus, we do not need to mention theories on unity any more.

Does that mean that every one of our people has fully come to realize the need to unite? That is doubtful. If we gather together all those people who shout unity, all those people who blame others for not uniting, all those people who admonish the society for building sides and fighting, we will have gathered several million people. It is strange that we don't have an organization made up of millions of those people. Maybe they want unity but push the responsibility onto others, not yet ready to get involved in the actual work of uniting.

We are made up of a body and four limbs, and if our body and limbs sever, we lose the ability to move around, we may even lose our lives. Likewise, if our society is made up of individuals, and if the individuals sever from each other, that society is as good as dead at that very moment. There is no point discussing anything further if we do not have any ability to unite.

When American colonists from thirteen states were getting ready to fight for their freedom and independence, they had to prepare food, weapons, and supplies. But the very first item they had to prepare was to plant the spirit of unity in everyone's head. They recognized the need for unity and devised a motto for everyone to recite, "United we stand, divided we fall."

We, too, need to take on the responsibility as owners and research the ways to unite and try to carry on with the work of uniting.

If I were to recite all the reasons why our ancestors couldn't unite in the past, and the reasons why we can't unite at present, and list all the proposed methods for uniting, it would be endless. So I would like to say a few things that I believe we need the most.

First, we establish a common wish list and conditions on which everyone can agree to act. The unity that we request for today is not one out of our emotions, but it is for the purpose of carrying out our work for the people. There are voices of opposition against emotional unity of any race of people, citing harmful effects against humanity in general. In asking for unity for the purpose of doing the work for our people, I am not discussing the rightness or wrongness of nationalism motivated by emotion. Whatever the race or nation, when they say "our nation," or "our race," it contains the natural tendency among such people to gravitate toward unity, so we do not need to emphasize that point any longer. What we need is an agreement on how we accomplish the unity in terms of common life and common endeavor.

The "unity for the purpose of doing the work of the people" will happen after we define exactly what it means and how we have to accomplish it. So we shouldn't blindly shout "Let's unite, let's unite," because that doesn't mean a thing, and there is no reason to ask for unity without knowing what to do to achieve it. We can name many examples throughout the history of the world in the past and at present that show the need for establishing the conditions commonly understood for the uniting process first before we can achieve the unity. We can find examples through our recent experience.

Thus, what are the conditions under which we can unite? The first answer is setting the objective. Second, we need to know how we are going to achieve that objective. Our objective is rather clear already, and we need not repeat it. We only need to agree on how we are going to do it. That is the common goal for our unity.

So, how do we establish the plans? It is up to every individual to come up with his own plans. You might say that if everyone has his own plan to offer, then we wouldn't be able to bring ourselves to unite because there are so many plans. But that is not so. As I pointed out earlier, a nation is made up of individuals, whose plans must come together to build a common plan. That is the unavoidable principle for our system.

Therefore, each individual must think and research for the solution for the present and future and present it for all of us to see. Then we shall form public opinions and let the process of "natural selection" and "survival of the fittest" take its course until we come to an opinion that is agreed upon by most people. That is the voice of the people, their will, and their command.

We are a nation of freedom, and we cannot treat the people like slaves. Our commands come from individual conscience and ideals, and we must not obey a certain individual or organization. Each one of us is the owner of our nation, and we should direct our questions to our conscience and ideals. And, because we are the owners, we don't need to behave like an employee who has to show off his accomplishment for rewards, we only want to do good for our nation. Therefore, we must respect our own thoughts and opinions as well as those of others and decide what is good for our nation regardless of where the idea came from, even ideas coming from those we do not like due to our personal feelings. If his idea is better than yours, you should gladly discard your own idea and adopt his as your own. You have had the experience of searching for the solutions as the genuine owner and therefore you appreciate what your counterpart has gone through to come up with his idea, and all you have to do is to choose the better one, that's all.

So, if we want to unite, we should focus on establishing suitable conditions for unity. If we are going to establish suitable conditions, you and I should go to the mountains or to a room with cool heads and begin to search for methods and plans. I dearly want everybody in every class not to ignore the task of establishing genuine solutions for our people, to avoid making abstract observations and abstract criticisms, to look deep inside you and think hard about detailed future plans. Then, present them for all of us to see and compare, and let the people determine by the rule of majority and accept the selected plan as the will of the people, and have all of the nation rally under one flag.

This is my deepest wish for our people to achieve as soon as possible.